pulp

martin aston

pulp

PAN BOOKS

First published 1996 by Pan
an imprint of Macmillan Publishers Ltd
25 Eccleston Place, London SW1W 9NF
and Basingstoke

Associated companies throughout the world

ISBN 0 330 34791 8

Photograph on page 208: Rankin

1 3 5 7 9 8 6 4 2

A CIP catalogue record for this book is available from
the British Library.

Typeset by Macmillan General Books Design Department
Printed and bound in Great Britain by
Mackays of Chatham plc, Chatham, Kent

Dedicated to Johnny Waller (1955–95)
whose initial faith in Pulp was finally rewarded,
and to Mat, whose initial faith should hopefully
get its just rewards.

acknowledgements

Thanks to Pulp for initial access; Geoff, Jeanette and Patsy at Rough Trade Management; Melissa Thompson and everyone else at Savage & Best PR; Tony Perrin and Simon Hinkler; Kate Molyneux and Billy Reeves for picture research assistance; Island Records press office; Clive and Bridget at Fire; Claire Evans at Pan; Ingrid Connell; those journalists whose quotes I borrowed. Special thanks to the Alexander family, Mat, Simon, Merle, Sara, Mark, Sanne, Kurt (you old Nazi), Meir, Yael, David P., Patrick, Gordon, Maxine, David B., Yvette, Rupert, Neal, Yas, Martin, Margriet, Gerrit, Emiel, Levi, Joanna, Stuart, The Boys In The Band. Extra special thanks to Angela, you're in a different class.

contents

contents

RUSSELL SENIOR:
'What's Sheffield like? It has a black, tongue-in-cheek
humour. It's self-deprecating, it lacks self-confidence and
yet, at the same time, it believes itself to be the
best in the world, if only at being ugly.'

STEVE MACKEY:
'My friend Steve and I always used to say that Jarvis
would be a complete star or he'd be a waster, sweeping
the streets for the next twenty years. Everyone knew
that in Sheffield. It was a fact.'

PULP

WHO THEY ARE
AND WHY YOU SHOULD
LISTEN TO THEM.

GROUPS, GROUPS, LIKE THOUSANDS OF DIRTY POTATOES THROWN INTO THE SAME SACK. HOW DO YOU TELL ONE FROM ANOTHER? IS IT WORTH THE EFFORT? THAT'S HOW IT IS NOWADAYS; A NEW ONE ON THE MARKET SHOUTING ITS VIRTUES AT THE TOP OF ITS VOICE. TOO MUCH NOISE. SO YOU GET SICK OF IT AND STOP LISTENING. FAIR ENOUGH.

SHOUTING ITS VIRTUES....

SO HERE'S ANOTHER GROUP. PULP. FROM SHEFFIELD. WANTING YOUR ATTENTION LIKE ALL THE REST. OFFERING YOU MUSIC. MUSIC THAT IS GOOD, YES **GOOD**. THERE ARE MANY WORDS I COULD USE BUT YOU WOULD PROBABLY HAVE HEARD THEM BEFORE. AT ONE TIME THEY MIGHT HAVE INTERESTED YOU BUT NOW THEY'VE HAD ALL THE JUICE SUCKED OUT OF THEM. SO WE'LL LEAVE IT AT GOOD, VERY GOOD IN FACT. ANYWAY, IF WORDS COULD DESCRIBE IT, WHY MAKE MUSIC? THIS IS WHAT ALL THE OTHERS CLAIM BUT NEVER DELIVER. FRESH AIR, BEAUTY, STUPIDITY, OWT YOU WANT, PAL; PULP GOT IT. O.K?

1

definitely a game of two halves

Once, the word 'pulp' simply denoted the succulent part of a fruit. The pith of the stem of a plant. The soft or fleshy part of an animal body. The inner substance of the tooth. Any soft, moist, slightly cohering mass, as of linen or wood, used in the making of paper. Then the word became synonymous with a style of postwar literature that sought the seedy truth about the underbelly of American society – the life of crime, the lure of lust, the search for kicks, the drive to escape. 'Pulp Fiction' was so called because the magazines and books were printed on low-grade recycled pulp paper, which matched the supposedly low-grade, immoral lifestyles between the book covers. 'Cheap', 'exploitative', 'sensational' and 'lurid' said the moral majority – but let's leave Jarvis Cocker's private life out of this for the time being, because we haven't mentioned Quentin Tarantino yet.

This canny, weasel-faced auteur has done his utmost to make 'pulp' the household-friendly word it is today – his cinematic *tour de force Pulp Fiction* has been the most talked-about film of the decade since its release in 1994. But as 1994 turned into 1995, a certain lean, gangly Oxfam-catwalking warbler became Britain's Most Wanted cultural icon, took over the magazine racks, invaded the gossip columns, and made fans of Prince William and a host of grandmothers who like their pop stars looking neat and tidy. Quentin hasn't quite managed to reach the same dizzy heights, although Jarvis Cocker and the pop group Pulp have had slightly longer to get around to it.

Sixteen years, in fact. Sixteen years which, in pop terms, is a painfully long stretch. Believe it or not, it was way back in 1978 that Jarvis and his three City Comprehensive, Sheffield schoolfriends started a pop group and christened it Pulp; that's not the same Pulp (of origins unknown, except that there were two members, vocalist Ann Bean and drummer Paul Burnell), which released a single called 'Low Flying Aircraft' in October 1979, but the same Pulp who soldiered on through different, mutating formations until consolidating the line-up that struggled for only another six years before flabbergasting fame and naked notoriety was theirs for the taking. If pop stars got points for perseverance, Jarvis Cocker would have been top of the league a long time ago.

And what a sixteen-year era it's been. Punk had given way to the New Wave by then, but throughout the movements of Two-Tone, New Romanticism, Hardcore, Rap, Post-hardcore, Acid House, House and Grunge (not forgetting Goth, Cowpunk and Shoegazing), there was nary a squeak out of Pulp on a populist level. They didn't make the singles and album charts until 1993.

Where had they been? OK, schoolboys rarely get it together enough to take on the world, so we'll pick 1981 as Pulp's 'Year Zero'. Even so, by 1985, the press and Jarvis were already conscious of the passing of time. An interview in the Sheffield *City Press* began with the suggestion that Pulp 'have been about to "break" for years. The big build up's happening again and it's probably their last chance. Things look promising this time, provided they don't fall out first.'

The optimism was misplaced, of course. But the *City Press* journalist was right in one respect – in pop, you usually only get one chance, at the most two. But Pulp seemed to have had several, and still kept coming back for more. Even if you didn't like Pulp – and many didn't – you had to admire their resilience.

I first met Jarvis in early 1986. We sat in my kitchen, on a typically damp day, the light fading fast. Dressed in regimental shades of grey but topped by a fantastic fake fur overcoat, he was struggling to summon up some enthusiasm, despite being asked to discuss Pulp's excellence as part of a 'State Of British Pop' article (Brit-pop was just a twinkle in the eyes of trendmongers). I was championing Pulp (I was also championing The Shop Assistants but never mind) though the music press was – rightly – putting its money down on groups like The Wedding Present, against whom Pulp were runts of the litter, the freaks with the violin, the doomy songs and the cacky stage decorations. Those who loved Pulp did so with near-religious fervour, though Jarvis was in a what's-the-point? mood the day of our interview, and the on-stage humour which pepped up the musical intensity of Pulp's live shows was noticeably absent. The lack of acceptance across the board was definitely showing signs of getting to him.

In another rare but rabidly appreciative article in *Melody Maker* the same week, Jarvis was asked where he thought Pulp would be in five years' time. 'I don't really like old bands,' was his immediate response, an ironic one given the eventual turnout. With a shrug of those stooped shoulders, he reckoned he'd either become a feature at Sheffield's infamous 'Hole In The Road' (the open-topped part of an underground subway leading to the city centre and a noted hang-out for tramps and drunks 'armed with a cider bottle in a brown paper bag') or he would be well-off somewhere. 'Either very happy or very depressed,' he concluded. 'I won't be in the middle.'

'There are only two options,' Russell Senior piped up. 'You're either a pop star or you're scrubbing crabs.'

2

space, the only frontier

Jarvis: 'I was convinced when I was younger that I didn't need a bicycle because I'd be whizzing down the shops with my personal jetpack, or I'd be living on another planet. You wouldn't need a bike if you were living on the moon: it would float away. I used to buy space annuals which said that by the 1980s, space stations would be orbiting the Earth and men would be colonizing Mars. I thought that I was going to become an astronaut.'

Come on down, Jarvis Branson Cocker – childhood stargazer, idiosyncratic outsider, imminent scribbler and fledgling superstar, born in Sheffield on 19 September 1963, in the suburb of Intake. Jarvis' parents Mack and Christine had already displayed artistic temperaments – his mother had taken a degree at art school while his dad was a jazz trombonist who enjoyed pretending he was, or was related to, Joe Cocker, Sheffield's venerated white blues singer (Joe used to enjoy the joke too and installed a gas fire in the Cocker household – a fact not known by many.).

Jarvis remembers them as bohemian types; sadly, his father displayed classic bohemian wanderlust, feeling constrained by an early marriage and domesticity, and eventually leaving home when Jarvis was seven. He moved to London and stayed out of contact until, four years later, he emigrated to Australia. The Cockers had believed Mack had killed himself, since they hadn't heard a word from him, until they were notified by an anonymous phone call that he was leaving the country. Christine had to give up her claims on bohemia and take up emptying fruit machines to support Jarvis and his five-year-old sister Saskia.

His father's departure was the second major blot on the landscape of young Jarvis's life. The first had been catching meningitis when he was five. Looking back, he realizes there was a good chance he could have died, as his school class had written letters 'and they wouldn't have gone to so much trouble if they didn't think I was on my way out'. When he recovered, his get-well gifts had to be destroyed in case of infection: 'I was left with a couple of cheap plastic spacemen who could be sterilized in boiling water.' Worse, the illness damaged his eyesight and forced him to don National Health glasses which, as any four-eyed get will tell you, cause much pointed mirth in the classroom and wincing embarrassment on behalf of the wearer.

No, childhood was never destined to be easy. 'I looked like an ugly girl,' Jarvis remembers. 'It was a normal Sheffield suburb, a bit rough maybe, but I was the only kid on the block with long hair, which my mum wouldn't cut. Long hair and skinny rib jumpers with really short shorts, as she made her own clothes, so it would look like a jumper dress.'

Worse, his uncle had married a German woman who would send over lederhosen-style leather shorts as gifts, which his thrift-conscious mother thought were suitably cute and sent Jarvis to school in them, upping the embarrassment. 'So I went to school looking like an extra from *Heidi*. Mortifying.' He would cajole his grandma into buying him normal shorts and then change on the way to school.

As if being christened Jarvis wasn't enough. Jarvis (which he was told meant 'spear carrier' – 'but I don't know about that') and Saskia may have been fashionably bohemian names but sounded poncy to down-to-earth Sheffield folk. Who knows what mental or physical cruelties were inflicted on this leather-chapped, bespectacled beanpole who was also forced to wear braces on his buck teeth, and be deemed a bit of a swot? No wonder outer space became a necessary escape from the quaking dimensions of inner space.

For the impressionable Jarvis, science fiction, more than pulp fiction, was where it was at. He was especially keen on Batman, wearing a cape, purple leggings and a mask on shopping expeditions with his mother. His first crush was on a puppet by the name of Marina, the aquatic beauty from *Stingray* (his mother even made him a Marina doll). His next object of desire was at least made of flesh and blood – Annette Firman from *Grange Hill*, the first in a line of independent, so-called 'badly behaved' girls that Jarvis took to fancying. He subsequently fancied the girl in the Aero ad but the first girl he ever kissed was a certain Caroline, in his early teens: 'We would never talk at school but I always ended up snogging her at parties.'

Like science fiction, pop slowly became a chosen means of expression and escape. Jarvis had imbibed his mother's record collection – 'mainly The Beatles, nothing all that exciting' – and started learning guitar at fourteen. 'Mum would say, "Come down here and have your tea. Stop all that plinky plonk." Though I never used to admit to liking music for some reason. I'd only listen to records when everybody was out of the house. I thought it was bad to admit that I liked it so I never actually bought records until I was quite old, until I got over that. I don't know why, as I became a bit of a music fiend.'

Looking back, Jarvis awkwardly recalls not being that bothered when his father left home – Saskia, by comparison, momentarily stopped going to school – but his subsequent behaviour revealed archetypal attention-seeking patterns. Out of place at school, he realized he couldn't be accepted by being sporty or just cool, so needing to deflect potential bullying – 'I did get fun poked at me, but not in a really nasty way' – he became a joker and prankster to elicit laughs and attract boy-acceptance and girl-interest. One time, he pretended to be dead, an effort he kept up for twenty minutes, during which time the school called an ambulance. Realizing that his fantasy had been all too convincing, he made a 'magic' recovery before it arrived.

Then, at fourteen, he started wearing his father's suits, possibly to accentuate his class loon/goon persona, perhaps as a subconscious way of stepping into his father's shoes (or just to get close to his memory), or simply because Jarvis was starting on the search for sartorial elegance that would one day help cement his reputation.

'I just realized that there was no way, even if I wore casuals, that I would be like everybody else,' he told *The Face*. 'It just never worked, it never looked good. So in the end, I thought if you have an imperfection, you may as well flaunt it and turn it into an advantage. If you have big feet, wear big shoes, if you're tall and skinny, wear very tight clothes.'

Jarvis had also discovered the legendary New York art-rock ensemble The Velvet Underground and their patron, artist and icon Andy Warhol. The New York group were a seminal influence on, and much bandied-about name by, punk stars as well as David Bowie and other art-rock/glam-pop luminaries. Making a virtue of your differences was a Warhol trait; to look paler, weirder, unique. Jarvis took to wearing high heels, and looking for unusual clothes in second-hand stalls and markets.

Dressing up and acting up – isn't that what all teenagers do? But it wasn't enough, and Jarvis started withdrawing into his own fantasy world. He used to imagine he had a camera inside his head that people could tune into and watch what he was doing: 'It was like starring in my own movie. Everything I did took on this incredibly dramatic perspective.' It was no real surprise, then, that Jarvis turned into a solitary, introspective creature. 'I hardly went out between fourteen and seventeen,' he freely admits. 'I went straight from my school to my room.'

His schoolfriend and fellow Pulp founder Peter Dalton remembers Jarvis as academically bright, keen on acting in school plays, 'and more or less the person he is today, though more insecure and alienated. He always used to turn up late for school, and walk into classes toward the end, because he couldn't get up in the morning. I think, like me, he felt that he was bored by the methods at school, whereby they take all the mystery and beauty out of a subject like English and render it as a series of blocks that you memorize to pass your exams.'

You can sense the escapist plots that bedroom must have hatched. Even by the age of twelve, Jarvis would imagine himself and his gaggle of schoolmates as a bona fide pop group, whether standing in the dinner queue or walking down the corridor, 'and all the kids were clapping us'. Not that this gangly Billy Liar let on about the feverish power of his fertile imagination – he had enough insecurities without incurring the dismissive wrath of his peers.

Yet three years later, in 1978, after punk culture officially seeped into the schoolyard, Mark Swift (drums), David Lockwood (bass), Peter Dalton (guitar) and Jarvis Cocker (vocals) had a pop group. 'Punk rock gave us the idea that anybody could do it, because 'none of us had any ability,' Jarvis recalls. The name of this particular idea was the cumbersome Arabacus Pulp, named after a coffee-bean commodity Jarvis had read about in the Share Index of the *Financial Times* during an economics lesson.

'I just wanted "Pulp" but I thought it wasn't enough on its own,' he reckoned. 'It was an unwieldy name and we knew it was rubbish, and no one understood the term anyway, so we dropped it after a year. People hated it and it was frequently spelt wrong. We've been billed as Pope And The Pulps before.'

Rehearsals began at Jarvis' grandmother's house. Her coal scuttle doubled as drums until a kit was donated by an old dance band via Jarvis' mother's boyfriend. His mum also put the band's name on the front of the bass drum in sticky tape.

The first song they mastered was the stone-cold classic 'House Of The Rising Sun', a huge hit for The Animals in 1963: 'it only had five chords, which were the first we had learnt to play,' Peter Dalton remembers. Being a woeful tale of sexual awakening, shame and despair, it was the perfect beginning for the documented life and times of a man whose words have expertly nailed our everyday experience of sexual awakening, shame and despair.

The group's first self-penned song was titled 'Shakespeare Rock', influenced by English classes, no doubt. 'It had embarrassingly awful words,' Peter Dalton thought. 'It started, "*I've got a baby, only one thing wrong, she quotes Shakespeare all day long,*" and later on, it went, "*all this Shakespeare makes me sick, she said, 'alas, poor Yorick'.*" I think we'd just done *Hamlet* at school.'

That effort was soon followed by 'Message To The Martians', which wasn't Jarvis' first lyrical trip into outer space because the song had no vocals, just some screams from David Lockwood, according to Peter Dalton's self-confessed unreliable memory. 'The track was a nine minute dirge, with the stolen bass line from Joy Division's "New Dawn Fades", 'Peter concludes, less than fondly. Then there was 'Disco Baby' (uncannily reminiscent of a title Jarvis would pen fifteen years later) and 'Queen Poser' – according to Peter, 'I think they were just two words we'd read in the *NME* and strung together, and not anything meaningful.'

Yet the first completed Pulp artefact was not a record but a silent Super-8 film, *The Three Spartans*, featuring Mark Swift, Peter Dalton and Jarvis, though since one held the camera, only two of them could be in the frame at once. 'A beanpole took over as the third Spartan,' says Peter. 'I remember Jarvis throwing it in the film. It wasn't much of an epic.'

The follow-up was *Spaghetti Western Meets Star Trek*, where Jarvis played Clint Eastwood (dream on, Jarv . . .) this time featuring voiceovers and a taped soundtrack. The group showed both films during school lunch-hour, charging 10p admission, making approximately £10, the first and last occasion Jarvis would make a profit for an unhealthily long time.

Before any songs could be unveiled, minor details needed adjusting. David Lockwood was thrown out for playing too fast:

'He thought it was a competition to see who could finish the song first, and then go off to the fridge to get something to eat, or to lie down,' Jarvis recalls. He was replaced by fellow schoolmate Philip Thompson. Meanwhile, Jarvis' grandma found the band's rehearsals too noisy so the boys plinky-plonked in the sitting room of the Cocker household instead. Before long, Pulp was staging its debut concert, held at school. They even tried to engineer a sense of occasion, but the piddly magnesium flares set off at the side of the stage failed so completely to mimic dry ice that the effect was never attempted again.

By 1980, Pulp had been diligent enough to fashion a local reputation beyond the schoolgates. A tape was sent to Marcus Featherby at local label Aardvark Records who didn't include Pulp in their *Bouquet Of Steel* compilation of Sheffield bands (steel being Sheffield's most lucrative export) but found room for them in the accompanying booklet.

Jarvis recalls that the blurb 'said something like, "a cross between Abba and The Fall"' which was quite apt. The comparison made sense since Jarvis' favoured Velvet Underground combined melodic subtlety (an Abba trait) with minimal rhythmic grit (a Fall trait). The Doors were another musical favourite – 'I liked bands with keyboards' – while more New Wave-contemporary approvals included American art-pop deviants Devo, Manchester's dark and doleful Joy Division and Liverpool's more sprightly, neo-psychedelic rivals Echo & The Bunnymen and The Teardrop Explodes.

Jarvis: 'Marcus started taking us under his wing, and though he seemed to be a strange and dodgy character, it worked out well for us, otherwise we wouldn't have known how to go about getting concerts because we were too young to get into pubs. We wouldn't have existed without him.'

Marcus Featherby helped get Pulp their first live show, at Rotherham Arts Centre on 5 July 1980. Peter Dalton: 'It was a weird venue, a bit like a gym, with a wooden floor and fold-down seats. We hardly had any equipment so we had to borrow it off another band that were playing.'

The group had already turned up in a mobile grocer's van, borrowed from a bloke who lived across the yard. There are no highpoints or disasters on record, and Peter Dalton remembers a reasonable response from the thirty or so members of the audience, as well as an approach from the man who booked shows at the Hallamshire pub. 'He came up after and offered us a show. I said, "Why, do you think we're good?" and he said, "No, I thought you were crap but I think people will like you." At least he was being honest.'

Yet, a month later, with new drummer Jimmy Sellers slotted into place due to slightly improved playing ability, the group made its debut in Sheffield at The Leadmill Club instead. In the days before it was associated with the local council, the venue was being squatted, and those in charge were staging an all-day festival. Pulp were second from the bottom of the bill. They turned up, asking, in earnest, where the gear was. 'We thought you just plugged in,' Jarvis confessed. 'People found us funny because we couldn't play very well. We were trying to be pop but it was all a bit punkish.'

Russell Senior, a Sheffield native but then taking Business Studies at Bath University, was in the Leadmill audience. He subsequently gave Pulp their first published review in his fanzine *The Bath Banker*, the same name that he had given to his own band – 'they were dreadful', he now admits. But 'Pulp were raucous and fun with wit and humour. They did a funny version of "(I'm Not Your) Stepping Stone" [a track first recorded by The Monkees but made famous by The Sex Pistols] and the bassist fell offstage during it, which was all highly amusing.'

The fall from grace was due to feedback from Philip Thompson's amp. As he walked away in an attempt to make it stop, he eventually ran out of stage. 'It was the first time any of us had encountered feedback,' Jarvis told *Record Collector*. 'We'd been playing through the record player at home and could never use amps because the neighbours would complain.'

John Quinn, who went on to become pop reporter for the *Sheffield Star*, first saw Pulp live in 1981, at the Marples pub. 'I'd been told about the band and then had a big argument with my dad about going to a pub, but I went anyway. I remember this ugly, tall singer, who was brilliant. Musically, they were OK for the time, but something about them stood out, as did his hair. He was hilarious too, putting on a mock-sincere voice, saying stuff like, "This is for my girlfriend who left me alone in the room over the front garage." Someone threw a wet toilet roll at one point, and it hit Jarvis in the face. A lot of singers would be upset but he just laughed.'

Martin Lilliker, John Quinn's predecessor at the *Sheffield Star*, remembers Pulp concerts, usually held at the cramped Hallamshire pub, where band members would stand on the tables, still playing, while audiences took delight in taking the piss out of Jarvis. He didn't always take the abuse that well. At a show at the George IV pub, Jarvis burst into tears because the crowd were laughing at him. 'Just because he stood out,' says Quinn. 'He ran off the stage and hid under the table.'

Martin Lilliker: 'He could take things to heart. I don't think people realized how sensitive he was. Despite his persona, he always wanted to be taken seriously, and when you're that young, people don't, and he obviously couldn't handle it.'

As Jarvis noted in later life, 'The raw materials I was dealt with at birth had me marked out for a *Blockbusters* contestant.' Yet he became a figure of popularity in spite of, or perhaps because of, his awkwardness. John Quinn and his friend started writing Jarvis Cocker's name on the toilet wall, which resulted in the headmistress, at school assembly, asking who this Jarvis Cocker was. We started writing Jarvis Cocker graffiti all over the place, which wasn't grown up behaviour but quite funny at the age of sixteen.'

Jarvis' name was also chanted on the school bus, and the attention must surely have boosted his confidence. He slowly evolved into what your mother would call 'a right character', yet Jarvis' mother felt forced to take steps, getting him a Saturday job at the local fishmongers 'in an attempt to make me more extrovert'.

It wasn't the most popular move with the girls; Jarvis recalls scrubbing down after work and still not getting rid of the smell. Yet he did meet his first girlfriend through the job. She worked in frozen food, two stalls down.

The fishmonger's was also where Russell first met Jarvis. 'He had a very convincing patter for selling fish, with lots of sexual innuendo around it. People would ask, "Have you got any crabs on you, cock?", and he'd say, "Ooh, missus, the trouble with me," and scratch himself, or, "I've got a lovely piece of tail end for your husband, love." He was one of the best performing fishmongers I'd ever seen.'

Russell subsequently put Pulp on in Bath, their first concert out of Sheffield, alongside their Sheffield peers New Model Soldiers. Peter Dalton remembers a pissed-up student audience, 'who were quite into us, so it was our best response to date', but it wasn't to end well. According to Russell, 'It ended in a riot because the bouncer got punched after all these punks arrived who didn't take kindly to all this racket. I was nearly expelled as a result.'

Two shows later, sixteen-year old Jamie Pinchbeck (once in local combo Satan) and fourteen-year-old Wayne Furniss were in on bass and drums respectively, having marginally better skills than their predecessors, though Peter Dalton remembers overhearing Jimmy Sellers telling someone, 'that we were just a sixth form band, which was bollocks, the rest of us were dead serious, and his comments were an affront to our dreams'.

Jamie was a friend from City Comprehensive while Wayne was attending the rival Frechville School down the road. Wayne was two years younger than the rest, but already playing guitar for Vector 77. Jarvis had met him at the *Sheffield Star*'s annual Search For A Star competition; the singer reckoned the judging was crap but the hospitality compensated. Something must have clicked between the members of the new line-up as Pulp soon landed a respectable support slot to Barnsley's emerging goth-rockers Danse Society at Sheffield's Limit club. It was a major confidence boost, and Pulp felt they were ready to make a demo.

In doing so, they approached another local eccentric, fifty-five-year-old musician Keith Patten. He had a home studio in nearby Darnall, and claimed to have invented the Vocoder in 1950 (the musical device which renders the voice like a squeaky robot, deployed by 70s entities like Electric Light Orchestra and Peter Frampton). With new songs written mainly by Jarvis with a little assistance from Peter Dalton, the band subsequently recorded 'What Do You Say?', 'Please Don't Worry', 'Wishful Thinking' and 'Turkey Mambo Momma' in Patten's bedroom.

Jarvis thought the finished tracks were 'too smoothie', but his voice was revealed to be good for his age, able to stay in pitch, with a rounded, warm resonance to it. The tape was put to immediate good use when Jarvis plucked up the courage to hand one over to DJ guru John Peel, who was doing a roadshow at Sheffield Polytechnic. Peel said he would listen to it on the way home but Jarvis didn't really believe him and was gobsmacked when the DJ phoned, speaking to his mother as Jarvis was still at school, and offered Pulp a session.

On 7 November 1981, in the BBC's West London Studios, Pulp recorded four tracks. When Jarvis was interviewed by John Peel in 1995, he reminisced about lacking the proper equipment ('the synth-drum was made out of an old electronic calculator case attached to a rubber burglar alarm mat, making this stupid noise'), borrowing a bass amp and not knowing what a graphic equalizer was, or how to make it work, so there was hardly any bass on the session. Today, Jarvis finds the session 'intensely embarrassing. I hope it doesn't ever come out.'

Yet the signs were encouraging. For starters, the curiously titled 'Turkey Mambo Momma' was Devo-esque, punky but tuneful, with fast, xylophone-toned keyboards and brass sounds: *'I was looking for the answer and the answer was you,'* Jarvis warbles.

'Refuse To Be Blind' was another slice of taut New Wave, with more wobbly synth sounds and tempo changes, over which Jarvis sung, *'They told me that I have got to relinquish these things that just fell out of my mind/ it's not that I am going crazy, it's just that I refuse to be blind.'*

'Please Don't Worry' was the poppiest of the four, with Jarvis' neat observation, *'think of all the money that's gone to your waist.'* 'Wishful Thinking' was the slow, courtly ballad, with another Joy Division-style bassline.

When the tape was re-broadcast in 1995, Jarvis told John Peel, 'it sounded like I'm trying too hard. It's like a bit of poetry you wrote when you're seventeen, and you always try and say everything about the world in three sentences.'

It was an accomplished enough debut for a bunch of naive teens, and the session was broadcast twice. It may have been ten years before Pulp were 'in session' again on BBC radio and thirteen years before they recorded another Peel session but this one made them stars at school, and local celebrities too, as the *Sheffield Star* put a Pulp photo and caption on the front page. The paper failed to persuade the band to pose in their school uniform: 'We were awkward even then,' Jarvis notes. 'At the time, we were the youngest, most precocious people around Sheffield.'

A subsequent call from London-based indie Statik Records requested a track for their forthcoming compilation *Your Secret's Safe With Us*. With no money available to record anything new, Pulp offered the demo version of 'What Do You Say?', the only track they didn't re-record for the Peel session: the track concludes, *'And now it takes up all my time/this face that is not mine/and so I rest my case/I don't want another's face''*. Says Jarvis, 'It was good to be asked but Statik certainly showed no interest in us after it was released.'

Yet it was a camera-lights-action! shift forward. It helped Pulp make their debut in the weekly music press. Pete Scott of *Sounds* (the now-defunct weekly rival of *Melody Maker* and *NME*) saw the group play the Marples, immediately noting Jarvis' skinniness ('the muscles of his brawny arms stand out like knots on cotton'). He also deployed the descriptions 'wilfully eccentric', 'fairground/carnival feel', and 'initially enjoyable but ultimately unfulfilling experience'.

The review made no mention of what had already become a Pulp trademark, the what-are-they-on? stage sets. Jarvis was keen on shows being 'events', to which end the stage was decorated with toilet rolls while two female dancers (rock + dance was a Velvet Underground effect), Amanda and sister Saskia, would throw toilet rolls, to give a streamers effect (like at football matches – hence the wet toilet roll thrown back at Jarvis), and cone hats for the band members that spelt out P – U – L – P (Devo were big on whacky hats). The band were also known to wear curtains, of the 1950s, floral variety, which Peter Dalton admits were stolen from the school library, and turned by Saskia into tops and trousers. Shows were advertised by Jarvis' A4 posters, with a logo of a praying mantis and the slogan 'There's No Substitute For Talent'.

'A lot of groups just go and stand there and don't do anything,' Jarvis told a local fanzine, who gratifyingly thought his effort 'immediately sets Pulp apart from other bands'.

Another Sheffield fan-rag pin-pointed the music, cynically observing that it seemed 'a mixed bag of all things modern, as if they listen to the John Peel show every night in an endless quest for influences'. The same writer also noted a penchant for '60s weirdness' – probably a reference to the way their immodest playing skills didn't stretch beyond a deployment of scratchy guitar and wayward organ that sat at odds with the era's New Romantic

Sheffield Sex City presents . . . *John Peel Show* **stars
make the cover of the** *Sheffield Telegraph* **in 1981 (***Left to right:***
Wayne Furniss, Jamie Pinchbeck, Jarvis Cocker, Peter Dalton)**
(*Sheffield Newspapers*)

pop sophisticates, electronic dabblers and anthemic rockers (including the now grown-up Bunnymen and Teardrop Explodes alongside the likes of U2). With no dance undertow, Pulp had little in common with Sheffield's particular brand of uptight funk or industrial percussion – groups like Test Department, Cabaret Voltaire, I'm So Hollow, Clock DVA and ABC.

The same fanzine showed concern for Pulp's fiction too. 'They don't seem to have seen enough of life to be obsessed with doom and despair, instead covering more superficial subjects such as "Message From The Martians" and "Disco Baby",' was the suggestion. Jarvis agreed, to an extent. Despite it being the golden age of dole culture, Falklands War crisis and the entrenchment of Margaret Thatcher, he recognized that Pulp had little social comment, but unless he could add something original to the political-pop agenda, he argued, what was the point?

Pulp were always going to follow Jarvis' singular ideal of living rather than slavishly follow trends. That singularity was already in place on the fashion front, as the first published *Sheffield Star* photo showed: Jarvis with hand-in-socket hairdo (the long hair of old was a distant memory, as, in New Wave mode, his upwards mop followed in the hair-steps of Bunnymen singer Ian McCulloch's bird's nest), a drab tank top, and those black-rimmed glasses – a collective look resembling a cross between Woody Allen and a giraffe. A nerd, in other words. 'The singer wins my nomination for any snappy dresser of the month award going, in faded pink trousers, pukey green shirt, suede jacket, glasses and dorky non-hairdo', one fanzine writer enthused.

'Jarvis was always finding shades of mustard that other people didn't even know existed, and someone shouldn't have invented,' Russell ventures. 'He's always remained true to himself.'

Jarvis then proceeded to exaggerate his supposed 'bad features' and play on his uniqueness, with mixed results. 'Believing in the punk spirit of individuality and self-expression,' Jarvis told *Select*, 'I attended a Stranglers show in a jumble-sale jacket and a blue tie my mother had crocheted for me. And all these people in Mohicans took the piss and said I was a mod.'

The rest of Pulp wouldn't have escaped suspicious looks either. The *Sheffield Star* photo has Wayne Furniss in a bow tie and striped suit trousers and Peter Dalton in a mis-matched suit jacket and trousers, topped by a fedora hat, worryingly tilted to one side: 'It was the time of Heaven 17 and ABC, when everyone wore suits. But I never wore the hat out because I was too embarrassed.'

In these hands, the Suburban New Wave look was potentially risky but at least there was no hint of New Romantic Naff. Fortunately, Jarvis had no truck with New Romantic fashion – 'I would have looked like a tit in knickerbockers,' he reckoned. Yet in a city like Sheffield, the only places where people could comfortably dress up and be themselves were the New Romantic and gay clubs.

Jarvis: 'What with Sheffield's ridiculous club policy, there were a small number of clubs to begin with, so there were only one or two places safe to go. One was Penny's, a gay bar that was a bit of a New Romantic club, with a good mixture of people and some good sights to be seen. But I was pretty conservative compared to most. I'd been wearing my dad's old clothes but they were four sizes too big for me, and I had a suede-fronted cardigan and a few things I got from jumbles, but I wasn't very outrageous.'

Yet he was outrageous enough to offend the ladd-itude of mainstream Sheffield. 'That's what "Mis-Shapes" is specifically about. Everyone in Sheffield socializes in the centre of town so you get these big packs of blokes, all dressed the same in white shortsleeved shirts, black trousers and loafers, and if you look a bit different, they'll call you a queer or run after you and want to smack you 'cos they don't like your jacket. I personally didn't get that much violence. The worst thing was getting kebab-ed on a late night bus. I was waiting on my own for a bus outside the cathedral, after nightclubbing, when a gang arrived. I had a plastic mac on, and the ringleader's opening gambit was, "Oh, thought you were a bag of rubbish left out for the bin." My bus arrived but I made the grave error of telling them to fuck off and forgetting the bus waits 15 minutes before leaving, so the ringleader got on and thrust his half eaten kebab in my face. I went home, and you know what a stink kebabs have, with bits of shredded lettuce over me, and my contact lens kind of slipped behind my eye.'

Peter Dalton: 'We used to go out drinking at the Hallamshire, where all the musos and trendies hung out. The pub was on West Street, the main drinking street in Sheffield, and the townies would go, "Let's go into the Hallamshire and look at all't weirdos."'

For the time being, Cocker also faced personal animosity on stage. The toilet rolls and general jumble-sale demeanour were soliciting crowd titters more than awe, and if the intent was a music/dance dynamic inspired by The Velvet Underground, it wasn't really working. Anyway, in those clothes, Pulp were more the Viscose Underground. Jarvis obviously wanted to be taken seriously but fanzine reviews would describe Pulp as 'ramshackle, endearing and daft'. At one show, it was the turn of Saskia to fall off the stage, wrapped in toilet paper. Evidently the world simply wasn't ready for a group touting faded pink trousers and a surfeit of Andrex.

3

university challenge

Def Leppard, The Thompson Twins, The Human League, Heaven 17, The Comsat Angels, Hula, Chakk, In The Nursery. More names to add to Sheffield's roll of honour, who had, or were about to, make a name for themselves. But the Sheffield scene was slowly evolving as the 80s progressed, and the change was not really for the better.

'Sheffield was a brilliant place to play, with a good scene going, but it all started going downhill when The Human League and ABC started charting,' remembers Simon Hinkler, guitarist in Sheffield's once fancied art-rock oddities Artery. 'The scene got less inventive and younger bands who looked up to them started doing more electro-pop stuff.'

A dearth of new talent is reflected in the fact that, out of the fifteen local groups which played the 'Dolebusters' protest concert against mass unemployment in 1985, Pulp are the only ones whose name you would recognize today. It wasn't really a lack of opportunity either, as local bands could win reasonable attendances at venues like the Broadfield, the George IV (also known as the Blitz), the Marples, the Royal (known under the unlikely name of the Ritblat Tube), Bar 2 at the university and the Hallamshire Hotel. Whether just fussy or keeping admirably high standards, Jarvis reckoned the Hallamshire on West Street (the main artery from the university to town) was the only decent Sheffield venue; it was also where all the local groups would hang out, being near some sought-after rehearsal space.

That said, the Hallamshire couldn't afford a music licence at one point, so Pulp played acoustic shows to get round the problem. 'We also got fed up with playing loud so we went easy listening for a while,' Jarvis explained. The transition from punky pop to acoustic pop was helped by the fact that Pulp as they existed then was coming to an end. In July 1982, members were leaving school, with Peter Dalton and Jamie Pinchbeck heading off to university, while Wayne Furniss had two years of school left and so slowly drifted out of the picture.

Peter Dalton proceeded to study law at Nottingham, although he had wanted to stay in Pulp, but his headmaster dad put paid to that, although the story that he picked up his dinner and threw it at Peter when his son put his plans to him is sadly the stuff of local myth. 'The band was the most important thing in my life at the time. It was a pretty horrible split, and quite a personal one too. I know Jarvis felt let down, and our friendship suffered as a result.'

For Jarvis, Pulp were still his reason for breathing, his tenuous hold on reality. He told his mother that the nationally broadcast Peel session showed what could be achieved, so she agreed to let him defer his place to do English at Liverpool University. (Despite the daydreams and distractions, Jarvis' brain had pulled him through: he'd even won the sixth-form reading prize and only flunked his Oxbridge entrance by pretending to the board he'd read a Thomas Hardy novel which he patently had not.)

'I didn't go to university because I wanted to do something for myself rather than just do what others had done,' he told me in 1986. Why was music so important, I asked? 'I don't know – it's hard to put your finger on why. I just feel compelled to do it. I didn't feel I had the choice. It's like all that crap you hear about music being in your blood, but I suppose it is. You believe something for a long time, so you tend to carry on without really knowing why. And recently I *have* been wondering why. I sometimes think I'd be better off not doing music because of the amount of worry it gives me.'

Back in 1982, however, he was keen as mustard. But in order

to proceed, Jarvis needed a band, and so he turned to Simon Hinkler. Artery was the first group Jarvis had ever seen live, and the quartet were probably Pulp's closest spiritual peers in Sheffield. The two groups also now shared a manager in Tony Perrin.

A hard-working figure on the Sheffield scene, Perrin had first seen Pulp supporting Artery at Sheffield Leadmill, and was instantly smitten. 'From the first song, Jarvis was a star. If not, then definitely a character. He acted the same way he does today. He had a wicked sense of humour but spoke too much between songs, which interrupted the flow of the set. But the Peel session really woke me up to the music, and the fact he could sing. They probably sounded closer to the way they do today than the configurations they went through between.

'My fondest memories of Jarvis are sitting in his mum's kitchen, at all hours of the morning, drinking tea, him having us in tears all night long telling us stories, just talking. That and kipping out on the hill overlooking Sheffield, tripping on magic mushrooms, tuning in to Radio Moscow and watching the satellites going overhead, convinced that we could hear the city humming, freezing to death and trying to get a fire lit. We just managed with our last remaining match, when some Hell's Angels went by, and we got into such a panic, we stamped it out. It was too dark to walk home, you see, so we had to wait for the first light. Jarvis was, as he is now, into experiencing things. He was just out of school, enjoying his first burst of freedom, just discovering himself.'

Perrin was impressed enough to offer his management skills, and then promptly offered to use the cash he'd made in the flyposting trade so that Pulp could record a mini-album, which the Northern indie distributor Red Rhino agreed to release on its own label. After recording some demos in August 1982, Jarvis and Simon rounded up a coterie of friends that consisted of Simon's brother David, local musician Peter Boam (Jarvis had asked him to be Pulp's drummer when Wayne Furniss wanted to transfer over to guitar, although Boam considered himself a poor drummer, and only ever played them live once, at the Crucible) and Artery drummer Garry Wilson (credited on the sleeve, to his chagrin, Simon recalls, under the pseudonym Beefy GarryO, awarded for his bear-like appearance). Wayne Furniss played guitar on one track, Philip Thompson's father Barry played some clarinet and flute, Saskia and Jill Taylor (who Jarvis later admitted to 'desperately fancying') added backing vocals while a trio of friends, Joanne, Julie and Alison, got a first-name credit for adding some conversational babble to 'Blue Girls'.

The team entered the local, antiquated Victoria Studios, situated in an old factory, a low-budget choice for the obvious reasons. The sessions ran smoothly enough, with Simon Hinkler producing, although the studio owner insisted they use his much-loved microphone which he claimed once belonged to Cliff Richard. 'He insisted on using it all the time too, on every instrument,' Jarvis grumbled.

Abandoning other early songs like 'How Could You Leave Me?', 'Why Live?', 'Teen Angst', 'Barefoot In The Park', 'Sickly Grin' and 'In The Heat Of The Day', Pulp made their singular debut in April 1983 with 'My Lighthouse', its artwork a Zen-simple rendition of three little fishies. Jarvis was probably aware of the title's potentially phallic imagery; in truth, the lyrics were inspired by a central image in the sublime French film *Diva* that was bewitching art-house cinemas at the time. '*It may seem strange to talk of love and then lighthouses but it's not strange to me,*' ran the chorus over a soaring, plangent melody, co-written by Jarvis and Simon. The B-side 'Looking For Life' was another lilting, jangling affair.

Pulp subsequently released the seven-track *It* album in April 1983. The title was a sad pun on the word 'pulpit', derived from the idea of preaching to people, while Jarvis admitted that the musical tone was inspired by the venerated American singer-

Just look at my hair . . . Jarvis on stage after the release of *It*, 1983
(Pete Hill)

songwriter/poet Leonard Cohen, 'with acoustic instruments and quiet female backing vocals. We were definitely anti-rock at the time.' Jarvis' voice had noticeably deepened too, though not quite to Cohenesque depths.

He might have intended to create a mood of poetic sobriety, influenced by Cohen's bedsitter introspection and the soft, narcotic side of The Velvet Underground mixed with aspects of The Teardrop Explodes' acid-folk but Jarvis' definitively Northern brogue aside, the end result was too effete and precious, too 'Indie MOR', closer to an American soft-rock breeziness or the winsome folkiness of Everything But The Girl.

According to Peter Boam, the new band had no time to rehearse before being thrown into making an album. 'There wasn't enough time for things to gell, and to cap it all, we were recording in the shittiest studio known to mankind, which Tony should have been shot for. Jarvis had an idea of what he wanted to do, something very psychedelic as he was listening to the Velvets, but he didn't have the language to make that leap. He was a bit of a John Lennon character in that he had good ideas but couldn't play them very well. Simon was on a piano tuning course and couldn't spend enough time to do anything. Jarvis asked me to work on some arrangements but all the ideas went out the window because Simon was the senior sideman. I ended up feigning flu and not turning up because it was Simon's show. He was into David Bowie's *Hunky Dory* and stuff like that at the time. John Peel wouldn't touch the album, which I think was a good move.'

Today, Russell reckons *It* was 'a fair document of puberty', which helps explain why Jarvis holds no little amount of animosity toward his first born. Who, after all, wants to re-embrace a time of virginal innocence? 'Pretty, naive and embarrassing,' he opined a couple of years after it was released, and true enough, the album is as awkward as a gangly, speccy, virginal eighteen-year old. Lyrics such as '*Crouched down behind a bush at the roadside I watch as you pass me by*' (from 'Blue Girls') were atmospheric (and an early sign of Jarvis' voyeuristic settings). '*The moon was dark, those clothes were tight / her perfume strong, it turned me on*' (from 'Wishful Thinking') was bearable but 'Love Love' was truly awful. With a horrible ersatz New Orleans ragtime feel behind them, the words '*I thought so long, then realized, that I love love*' and the terribly twee admission of going to '*the pond to feed the ducks on bread*' – suggested Jarvis ought to get a life.

Many years later, in *Record Collector*, Jarvis thought *It* was 'like somebody on a diving board, about to jump. In fact, there's a song we recorded but never mixed, 'Sink Or Swim', about standing on the threshold of life. They're all love songs but from the perspective of not knowing about it as I'd never had a girlfriend.'

For all its naivety, *It* had its fair share of lush melody and charm, especially 'My Lighthouse' (which opened the album), 'Wishful Thinking', 'Boats And Planes' and 'Blue Girl'. What's more, the confessional tenderness, romantic disaffection ('*I'd like to turn you over, see what's on your other side / see if the problem's in my mind*'), and see-sawing folk-pop temperaments actually predated The Smiths, especially 'Joking Aside' and 'In Many Ways'.

Relaxation at home, the Jarvis way, April 1983

(*Zbysiu Rodasin*)

For Jarvis, though, lush meant slush. 'I was hankering after something which I didn't have any experience of, and when you're crying for something for a long time, sometimes you find that you don't want it and chuck it in the bin,' he reflected soon after. 'I suppose I'm a bit more cynical than I used to be, although I don't want to be because I don't think anything good can come of cynicism. You just drag things down and don't take any chances.'

The *NME* mercilessly slagged *It*; *Melody Maker* simply ignored the album. *Sounds* staffer Dave McCullough was alone in reacting favourably. 'A brave attempt to make this year's cult album,' he ventured, but concluded, '*It* finally fails because it puts style above content.' This was a criticism easily levelled at McCullough's review, which made a big deal out of the music's supposed influences, referring to the 'smoothie' sounds of The Mamas and Papas and Simon & Garfunkel, though Jarvis didn't mind the comparison to 'classic' pop composers Jimmy Webb and Burt Bacharach.

'It was our middle of the road period,' Jarvis concluded. 'There was this music/musician type of thing going on, whereas later I became the best musician in the band and I'm not very good! When people know how to play their instruments, their imagination goes.' The *Sounds* review made him realize that he 'didn't want to be anyone else besides myself'.

The truth was, Jarvis felt he had been coerced by Simon Hinkler and Tony Perrin into making a softer-sounding record, though Perrin remembers it more as 'directing than forcing him. We all wanted the music to reach as wide an audience as possible, and since Jarvis wrote nice, melodic songs, Simon picked up on that and developed it.'

Worse still, Perrin encouraged Jarvis to write a commercial single in the style of Wham!, of all poles-apart peers. So it came to pass that in September, backed by the Hinkler brothers, Peter Boam and drummer Magnus Doyle (on loan from another local

Suits you, sir . . . a decorative Pulp on stage in Sheffield in 1983.
(*Left to right:* **Peter Boam, David Hinkler, Jarvis Cocker,**
Tim Allcard, Magnus Doyle)
(*Zbysiu Rodasin*)

combo, Midnight Choir), 'Everybody's Problem' was released. The problem remained Pulp's alone, with its inexpert jauntiness, parping trombone and wobbly vocal. 'As soon as I'd written it, I realized I'd made a grave error,' Jarvis admitted. 'What's more, the vocal was a guide track – I messed up all the words.'

'Unmemorable lightweight, fey drivel,' *Sounds* snorted this time. 'Their skulls deserve to be crushed like eggshells.' Pulp were suitably crushed by their sales. 'My Lighthouse' sold 150 copies while *It* managed a massive 300, as did 'Everybody's Problem'. 'Needless to say,' Tony Perrin realized, 'Red Rhino weren't particularly motivated to carry on. For some reason, Pulp were the most un-credible group in the world, a whimsical semi-acoustic outfit from up North with a crap name. You needed to see them live to get what they were all about but they didn't have the profile to get the press out to see them.'

Just before the release of 'Everybody's Problem', Peter Boam remembers turning up for a rehearsal to find that Simon had left.

The group publicity photo at the time featured just Jarvis, sister Saskia and Tim Allcard, a member of local band In A Bell Jar. Almost as if to signal a new phase, Jarvis had decided to grow a goatee beard. 'I don't know why I ever did, as I used to get the piss taken out of me at the fishmonger's,' he told *Record Collector*. 'But I found my dad's old student union card, when he was the same age as I was then, and he had the same beard. It scared me because I thought I was going to do the same as him, get married and then leave.'

Without Simon, Peter Boam says, 'It was almost as though Jarvis had been left without a rudder or a sense of direction. He needs someone who can mix his palette for him.' Boam was also unhappy about being left out of the publicity photo, and the fact that Jarvis had taken to inviting numerous people to join Pulp: 'Anyone, it seemed, who looked interesting. They might have been nice people perhaps, but one Crucible show had thirteen of us on stage, stretching to banging tambourines in the balcony. He and I weren't talking the same language, so I left my instruments with them for a year and picked them up later, and got into acting and theatre music. I wished I'd pursued things but I didn't. Anyway, it was better that they started off from scratch again, which Jarvis did.'

With Simon Hinkler off the scene, the rudderless Jarvis let off some necessary steam in several offshoot groups. There was Repressive Minority, Michael's Foot, a one-off Hallamshire event under the name The Jarvis Cocker Explosion Experience, and Heroes Of The Beach, whose band member Steve Genn brought a parents/children show to an uproarish end once when he pulled his trousers down. 'We were light-hearted to the extreme,' Genn recalls. 'We'd take the piss out of local characters. We also did a monumental mime to "Come On Eileen" once.'

Otherwise, a collective veil is drawn over all memory of those calamitous days. And over the stage play that would precip-itate the next chapter in Pulp's long and winding story . . .

4

the miners' strike changed my life

Enter the Bath Banker dragon. Once a member of heavy rockers Isengard (named after a valley in *Lord Of The Rings*), Russell Senior had thrown in his fanzine and group when he finished his Bath University degree and returned to Sheffield to begin anew. With jet-black hair, a wedge cut and staring eyes, Russell had real presence, with an uncanny resemblance to David Byrne of New York's artful New Wavers Talking Heads. He also held a real personal agenda; fired up by his artistic ventures at Bath, he was keen to make waves, which included the staging of a play he had written. Jarvis was to take the lead role, with various other Sheffield alumni in both acting and musical roles, including Tim Allcard, Magnus Doyle and Ellie Ford, a friend of Magnus' sister Candida.

According to its author, *Fruits Of Passion* was a Dadaist-influenced piece of agit-prop that climaxed with Jarvis eating a plate of dog shit at a job interview. As you do. 'There were sequences when you just left a hoover on until members of the audience started walking out . . . provocation was the name of the game at that point,' Russell emphasized. 'We proceeded to get bottled off everywhere.' In spite of it all they managed to complete four performances.

Against the odds, the trade weekly *Music Week* had called Pulp 'one of the best hopes for 1984', but there wasn't a band as such. Simon Hinkler had returned to Artery duties after a year at college but Jarvis decided to have 'a last ditch effort', and started rehearsing and writing with Russell on guitar and violin and Magnus on drums. They were soon joined by Magnus' friend Peter Mansell (nicknamed Manners) on bass and Tim Allcard on keyboards and between-song poetry.

Peter Mansell was only sixteen at the time, but chose to forego schoolgang pranks and the opportunity to work in Sheffield's famous steel cutlery factories for music. In an interview with *Record Collector*, Mansell reminisced about rehearsing in Jarvis' mum's garage: 'It was tiny, and full of all this shit amplification. The first time I went there was for an audition, and Jarvis was holding this little microphone against a cymbal. Russell was playing his Rosetta guitar with a bow. I thought, Bloody hell. This is nothing like *It*. I thought I'd be playing "My Lighthouse" and all those catchy songs.'

With Russell keen on a bit of provocation and Jarvis ready to expand after *It* – 'I thought, Fuck off, let's go to the other extreme' – it set the stage for Pulp to toughen up both sound and vision.

Russell: 'I'd liked the early Pulp but then it went all very poncy with *It*: I thought the album really dreadful and a bit of a sell-out, which I told Jarvis. My big concern was these big poncy, slushy ballads: I wanted to introduce this more hardline attitude. It was the time of the miner's strike, so there seemed like a need for more confrontational music than *"baby, I love you"*.'

The new songs, Russell reckoned, 'were more violent, more frustrated. There are some softer songs but there are no love songs any more. The word 'love' doesn't get used very often.' When the spirit of love was invoked, though, it was never done idealistically. 'It's more painful now,' Jarvis told *Sounds*. 'Grabbing, clutching and missing.' In other words, more Roman Polanski than Burt Bacharach.

Jarvis disliked the hard rock of the day – 'Noise is an easy thing to hide behind,' he sneered – but he admitted a liking for The Birthday Party, the Australian extremists who had stormed into the early 80s post-punk scene with a raw, visceral mix of rock and torchy blues. Another likely influence was Dig Vis Drill, a fellow Sheffield group Pulp had played shows with (Mr Morality made it a threesome) under the banner 'The Outrage Tour'. Dig Vis Drill was all dissonant, uncompromizing synth-noise ('Nine Inch Nails ten years before their time,' according to Rob Mitchell of Sheffield's premier dance label Warp), infused with strident left-wing politics. Like Russell, they actively supported the miners' strike. In the class 'war' that the strike precipitated, poncy ballads were the sound of reactionary conservatives.

Not that Pulp were keen to adopt a more typically Sheffield sound. They ridiculed the 'industrial' sound derived from the city's steel manufacturing base that had coloured the local music scene. 'When you go to Grimsby,' Jarvis figured, 'you don't expect fish-slapping, or the noise of trawlers.'

Russell: 'I played my dad Test Department and he said, "Well, I can hear that down the factory all day." We were on the other side, rehearsing among the factories and hearing all this racket going off, and not wanting to emulate it. We weren't students, we actually lived there, and wanted to make prettier music. But we were trying to be something really intense – bands around in Sheffield at the time that could be seen to be an influence, would be Cabaret Voltaire, Clock DVA, and personally I saw us in that tradition, although our music was totally different.'

The Sheffield band that Pulp, at least in their later incarnation, came to share aspects of sound and vision with, was The Human League, Sheffield's most successful pop group before Pulp, one which had mutated from awkward caterpillars to beautiful, chart-topping butterflies. When the first League line-up had split in half in 1980, one faction formed Heaven 17 while the dulcet-tonsilled Phil Oakey and Martin Wright employed two girls they'd found dancing in a disco, and *voilà*, you had a pop group working on numerous levels of cheesy magnificence and pop sophistication. (Vice-Versa would quickly do the same, when Martin Fry &

Co. became the gold-lamé-suited ABC. The Thompson Twins, and then Pulp were later to perform the same transitionary trick so it was obviously a Sheffield trait.)

Yet in one of those early fanzine interviews, Jarvis had confessed that he wanted to be a pop star 'but not like Phil Oakey'. Jarvis' initial feelings were probably professional jealousy as Russell remembers that Pulp respected the League 'for Phil Oakey's sense of humour and sense of irony. Our bugbear was that, in Sheffield, people thought that if there's irony, you can't be serious, which is nonsense. You can be totally serious about what you say though sending yourself up at the same time. Fortunately the world has moved on enough for that to be accepted, but it wasn't then, and we suffered for it.'

The new Pulp – the ironic but sincere model – were quickly put to the test when they debuted at Brunel University. With great courage they took the place of the smartly named Ivor Biggun & the Hairy Cocks, a band specializing in rugby songs. A friend had originally booked them for a show, then cancelled it in favour of the rugby band, a fact which Pulp chose to ignore. Ivor & Co. never turned up, which was the only factor in Pulp's favour that night. Besides the band's image – the cadaver-thin Jarvis, cadaver-faced Russell and weird-bearded Tim for starters – they got off to a less than flying start when the introductory sirens blew a fuse.

While that was being fixed, Tim Allcard's poetry went down worse than the proverbial lead balloon. When the music got going again, one of the audience expressed himself by mooning the band, whereupon Jarvis – the new confrontational, gonna-be-me model – unceremoniously kicked the offending arse. The MC tried to stop the show, so Jarvis wrestled him to the ground. In other words, another Russell/Pulp-related incident, another riot. The resulting stage invasion forced the band to bar themselves in the dressing room until it was safe. Confrontation was fine, but not if it involved personal risk (though Peter Boam remembers a show when a skinhead was baiting Jarvis, to which the singer responded by leaning forward and biting him on the top of his head – and lived to survive the day!).

Whether this alone was the catalyst – it was also believed that Tim's keyboard playing was the equal of his poetic appeal – Allcard left the group, to be replaced by Candida Doyle, Magnus' sister, Peter Mansell's girlfriend and dole-dweller at the time.

Diminutive, almost doll-like, but blessed with a much quirkier character than that clichéd description allows, the plastic jewellery-festooned Candida had seen Pulp numerous times in Sheffield, starting at the Royal pub. "I had a first date with this boy, but he was living with someone else so I couldn't sit with him as he was sitting with her! I'd read about Pulp and thought it wasn't my thing but they were really good, very different and powerful, with some really loud songs and others really nice. I liked lots of punk but also *Saturday Night Fever* and *Grease*.'

She joined because, she dimly remembers, 'Tim found it difficult playing in time. I'd had piano lessons so Mag and Pete suggested me. We jammed and I stayed.' Candida's first show was in London (at the Heywire Club), using a new keyboard bought by Tony Perrin. 'As far as I know, they're still using it today,' says Perrin. 'It was a big contraption with big knobs and half the keys didn't work. When they rehearsed at Jarvis' mum's house, they'd use a broom handle for a mike stand. Equipment was very sparse in those days.'

The concert was attended by Dave McCullough's fellow *Sounds* staffer and Pulp enthusiast, the late Johnny Waller (he was tragically killed in a car accident a month after contributing his comments to this book). Waller might have been too hungry to avoid leaving the show to grab a pizza but he still loved Pulp enough to want to work with them. Disillusioned with the increasingly influential Heavy Metal and Oi! factions within *Sounds*, Waller had begun fashioning a life outside of journalism, teaming up with London-based music publisher Clive Solomon in

Candida breaks a smile, thus spoiling Pulp's otherwise spotless
new image, 1984. (*Left to right:* Candida Doyle, Peter Mansell's
shadow, Russell Senior, Magnus Doyle, Jarvis Cocker)
(*David Bocking*)

order to form a record label. He put Pulp's name up for consideration.

Fire Records proved both Pulp's salvation and their damnation, through a relationship that lasted for nearly a decade. They were the only record label to believe in Pulp enough to put money on the table (as they would do with other innovative but not instant commercial propositions, like The Blue Aeroplanes, Spacemen 3 and Teenage Fan Club) but their independent status and working practices became an enormous frustration and burden to the group. 'I never liked Solomon but it was the only offer on the table,' Jarvis acknowledged. 'The only thing I can say in favour of them is that they gave us money to record.'

Pulp were first offered a publishing deal by Solomon's Twist & Shout imprint but, with Red Rhino out of the picture, a record deal was set up as well. Says Clive Solomon, 'Johnny had come into the office brandishing a copy of *It*, and I'd thought the songs and Jarvis' voice were wonderful, so we wanted to do something with this band.' The fact that Pulp had disowned *It* didn't bother him: 'I know they wanted to sound more rough and ready but I never thought in terms of signing someone after you hear new demos. If I hear something I love, I want to work with that band, not on what they do next.'

Russell sent out a letter with Pulp's newly completed demo that described the band as (all punctuation as written) 'huddled around the heater in the garage. The only noises were electric dronings: Happy Songs = bubblegum, Sad Songs = blank cynicism, Good songs, Bad Songs, Inbetween songs, too many songs . . . We thought, "the most meaningless thing in the world is to be a pop band". We turned to hit the metal objects around us and made a nasty noise – but the steel factories did it better. The question kept nagging, "Where's Truth & Beauty?"'

'Truth *is* beauty,' Jarvis claimed in our 1986 conflab. 'Sometimes truth is very ugly but if it's true, then it can't really help but be beautiful. Sometimes you can see a film that is pure rubbing-your-face-in-the-shit for the sake of it but other times it will do it with a point, which rings true, and then it doesn't matter, no matter what it's showing.'

As one fanzine writer astutely noted, Pulp had shifted ground 'from the politics of love to the politics of the soul'. On stage, they were doing the same, shifting towards the noise/dissonant side of The Velvet Underground as well as the creepy ballads. Clive Solomon remembers hearing tapes of VU-style jamming 'but just in a couple of things. They didn't go noisy, just weirder. They just wanted their pop music to stay melodic but sound darker.'

Tony Perrin supports the VU theory. 'Their performances then were almost performance art rather than concerts. They'd drafted in a strange character to recite poetry between shows, with mime – Jarvis was into the Andy Warhol, Factory concept, and everything the Velvets tagged onto their music. But their reaction against *It* mellowed by the time they entered the next phase, where they brought a sembance of structured order back into what they were doing.'

In May 1984, the band recorded a twelve-track demo, given the obscure title of *Sudan Gerri*. Two of the tracks, 'Coy Mistress' and 'I Want You', were included on *Company Classics No. 3*, a compilation cassette, before the Fire deal came into effect. When it came to releasing the first single on Fire, Pulp bypassed 'Srpski Jeb', 'Cousins', 'Take You Back' and 'Back in L.A.' ('A song about someone who gets a thrill out of being run over by the woman he is in love with,' Jarvis explained) for the uptempo 'Maureen'. They even made a cheap video for the track but Fire preferred 'Little Girl (With Blue Eyes)', a song Pulp continued to play right up until 1994.

'It was the standout song on the new demo tape, just magical,' Waller swooned. 'Every band has one classic song, which is nearly always a ballad, even if the band are rockabilly or noise-core. "Little Girl" was Pulp's true classic.'

Due to the inexperience of both group and label, business

**More suited sobriety: Pete 'Manners' Mansell (*left*) and Russell Senior
(*right*) shot for the *Little Girl (With Blue Eyes) EP*
(*David Bocking*)**

matters took almost a year to be finalized, and Pulp recorded
more demos in November. Jarvis existed on the dole; the nearest
he got to a proper job was a three-day week at an under-fives
resource centre, which he hated. But the group gave him hope.
He told *Melody Maker*, 'It gives you a centre to your life, gives
you an excuse to be alive, even if you're just fooling yourself and
there's not much chance of anything happening, because you
have a purpose.'

With Simon Hinkler in the producer's chair again, the group
eventually recorded 'Little Girl (With Blue Eyes)' in June 1985,
and released it as part of a four-track EP in the autumn. The
track was the clear proof of a new, fierce uniqueness. It was simultaneously morose and grey, colourful and vibrant, simultaneously
lush and tender, brooding and sinister. Marked by Russell's

In session for *Sounds* magazine. Peter Mansell plays Darth Vader
(*David Bocking*)

pizzicato violin and its slightly pilfered intro (from James &
Bobby Purify's 60s soul classic 'I'm Your Puppet'), 'Little Girl
(With Blue Eyes)' sounded like a small-scale Walker Brothers
(the fantastically moody, fantastically successful mid-60s trio who
specialized in heartbreak pop) or a British version of Jacques
Brel (a gut-wrenchingly poetic, socially conscious Belgian singer-
songwriter legend popularized in the UK by Walker Brothers'
lead vocalist Scott Walker after the trio split, and later by David
Bowie).

Better still, 'Little Girl' had a killer chorus: '*There's a hole in your
heart and one between your legs / you never have to wonder which one he's
going to fill in spite of what he says.*' Baby doll squeaks and Jarvis'
deeper intonations only compounded the disturbing mood.

Jarvis seemed uncomfortable about explaining the lyrics at the
time but admitted they concerned a girl getting pregnant, a
storyline inspired by seeing a picture of his mother getting out of
her wedding car, 'and realizing she was only twenty when she got
pregnant and had to get married. She was at art college but gave it
up to have me.'

'Little Girl' marked Jarvis' passage out of awkward, day-
dreaming adolescence. His virginity had been lost two years
earlier in 1983, mere months before his twentieth birthday ('I
was still a teenager, which made me happy'), on a patch of grass
in Weston Park, Sheffield, to a fellow virgin. His first major
relationship had begun a year or so later, though her name was
never disclosed in any interview (as continued to be the case with
all of Jarvis' girlfriends). The relationship, Jarvis said, 'started out
being quite innocent and got to being very traumatic without
either of us knowing why. In my naive days, I thought that
you were going to get a girlfriend and then it was all going to
be all right. And then you find out that it's not going to be all
right.'

Jarvis had got used to the thought that men and women were
basically the same, due to his upbringing in female company:

'My dad wasn't around and my grandad was sixty-odd and didn't really count, so I had my own "feminine" outlook,' he claims. When he realized the extent of the sex wars after that first relationship, it hit him hard.

The experience was bad for the heart but great for his art. As Johnny Waller reckoned, '"Little Girl" had a real sting in the tail. It was presented as a mushy romantic song but the lyrics are quite venomous. He was very astute at summoning up real emotions and giving them imaginative characters.'

Members of the press were equally thrilled. *Melody Maker* praised the 'slow motion nursery rhyme broodiness that swirls into alarming hiccuping noises like you're playing the record at the wrong speed.' *Sounds* enjoyed the 'tender sentiments, haunting melodies, nightmare visions and creepy vocal layers'. The *NME* reckoned it sounded 'like Leonard Cohen's *Greatest Hits* ate them', while Sheffield fanzine *Herring Aid* boldly called Jarvis 'a sort of Bacharach and David of the inner city'.

Its chorus ensured that 'Little Girl' was effectively banned from radioplay. Despite its 1 a.m. slot, even Radio Hallam's progressive pop show New Age Musak faded the track out after the chorus; the flabbergasted DJ announced, 'Well, I never expected anything like that from Pulp.' In Jarvis' view, there was no point in couching ideas in euphemisms anymore – honesty had to come before commerciality.

The B-sides gave even freer rein to Pulp's dark side. 'Simultaneous' sent Velvets-style shivers down the spine, with violin/keyboard drones and crashing interludes. 'Blue Glow' was a more conventionally rousing ballad, marked by an alternately jabbing and lulling violin and Jarvis' tremulous vocal that matched the sentiment of '*so late looking up at our window as it bathes me in your blue midnight glow . . . tonight, make it tonight.*'

If Russell had noticeably altered Pulp's sound, he was also to momentarily overhaul the group's psyche too – with potentially damaging consequences. Russell wrote and sung the last track,

Jarvis before the fall . . .
(*David Bocking*)

'The Will To Power', a title liberated from German director Leni Riefenstahl, whose Nazi propaganda film of the 1934 Nuremberg Rally, *Triumph Of The Will*, had explored the 'homo superior' beliefs of German philosopher Friedrich Nietzsche. '*1933, where are you now?*' Russell deadpans, but his broad Yorkshire accent made it almost comical. Less comical was the way the song managed to attract what Russell describes as 'a small but vociferous skinhead following'. The song was quickly dropped from their live set.

Russell: '"The Will to Power" was subject to much misunderstanding. It was written in 1983 when we were living in a real apathetic, SDP kind of environment, where nobody was taking sides. It was a plea for more polemicism and politics, for people to take sides. Like, where's the extremism? I was reading about class conflict in Germany at the time but I approached the song from a communist side, although I can see how it could mistakenly seem like a bit of a fascist song. If it is to be interpreted as anything other than a rampant stream of nonsense, then it should be as "let's get up the barricades and take sides and have a revolution," but we were on the left, not the right.'

The experience evidently unnerved Pulp enough for them never to forge a distinctly political song again, unless you count the suppressed anger at the heart of the 'class war' saga of 'Common People'. But while 'Common People' later sold 200,000 copies, 'Little Girl' sold well under 2000.

Johnny Waller: 'Pulp were disappointed, but they weren't naive yokels. They didn't think they would sign to Fire and make millions. Everyone was thinking more of good reviews and radio play on John Peel and Kid Jensen.'

In case the radio ban wasn't enough, Jarvis had managed to add injury to insult, putting a stop to any promotion altogether. Copying something he'd seen done a week earlier, he'd tried to impress a girl by walking around the outside window ledges on the second floor of the Sven Bookshop in Division Street. He was in the process of negotiating the distance to the next window ledge when he realized he wasn't going to make it.

'I said, "Do you want to see something quite interesting?", and she begged me not to do it but I was in the mood,' he recalled. 'It was just senseless bravado, which is quite out of character. I realised I didn't have the strength to do it, or to climb back in, so I had to count to three and just let go.' He might have dressed as Batman as a child but he cocked up as Spiderman as an adult . . .

Three must have been his unlucky number; three days before 'Little Girl' was released, Jarvis became the man who fell to earth. Passers-by reputedly stepped gingerly over his body, and off he went to Royal Hallamshire hospital, where the doctor diagnosed a fractured pelvis, broken wrist and ankle, a slight impediment to the task of acquiring pop stardom. He had to spend six weeks in the Royal Hallamshire hospital and numerous more in a wheel-chair. When the plaster-cast was removed, Jarvis was warned he might not walk properly again. 'The doctor said, "You do realize that the bones are very fragile?",' he told *Time Out*. ' "We've tried to put them back in place but it's impossible to do it properly, so you'll always have pain there. And in the end, you'll be in so much pain that we'll have to fuse your foot to your ankle."' But, the odd twinge aside, Jarvis confounded medical science.

There were hidden advantages to the incident, aside from a legitimate upstaging of Morrissey's claim for 'invalid' status after he wore a hearing aid on *Top Of The Pops*. More profoundly, Jarvis found the experience truly life-changing. 'It made me decide to live in the present and not the future, and gave me time to think about things. It made me realize I didn't have a guardian angel looking after me.'

Living in the present, and not the future, included the realization that the fantasies of the past should be left there. 'I finally realized that space was all a fantasy when I was twenty-two,' he admits. 'I didn't have any money and there wasn't much coming in from the band so I was selling off all my belongings.

Are we sitting comfortably?
The wheelchair-bound Jarvis on stage in Sheffield, 1985
(*David Bocking*)

I distinctly remember tramping around Sheffield with a yellow portable washing machine, trying to sell it to get the money for some food. It was pissing down and I thought to myself, "Jarvis, you were supposed to be living in space by now . . . you have to stop living your life for the future".'

Having a group could be as much an escape from banal reality as living on the moon. For example, Jarvis was unaccustomed to shopping because he reckoned that, one day, 'I'd have everything brought in'. Now he found himself going to supermarkets, checking the weather, 'things I had never done before. Before then, I used to get up in the afternoon and avoid the obstacles of the mundane everyday. I'd done nothing except live in the future. It was my countdown period. I saw myself as a rocket on the launch pad waiting to take off, but it went on indefinitely. I had been stuck in a ward with a lot of old blokes who'd worked down the pit and talking to them made me alter my viewpoint.'

The accident meant that Pulp played a measly two shows between the end of March and beginning of September, and ended up playing only thirteen during the whole year. When they did play, Jarvis was sat in his wheelchair, which provided helpful photo opportunities for the music press, but it was commonly presumed to be another of Pulp's theatrical devices, and therefore not in great taste. 'That was because you kept on getting up and walking off at the end of performances,' Russell suggested to Jarvis in a *Melody Maker* interview, though the singer has always maintained his innocence. Provocative as ever, Russell tried capitalizing on the incident but failed to persuade Jarvis to come onstage on a trolley with drip attached.

While 'Coy Mistress' and another new demo 'Anorexic Beauty' were released on a compilation from Pork Cuisine Records, *Beware The Bacon Slicer*, Pulp were at work on their new single. While in hospital – his mother brought him in a keyboard – Jarvis wrote 'Dogs Are Everywhere', which was recorded in February 1986 and released in May. The track set a lovely slice of lyrical misanthropy to a sublimely downbeat melody. Said the sleevenotes: 'Recent evidence shows that man is a direct descendant of the dog, rather than the ape, as had been previously believed. Some are closer to their roots than others.'

Like 'Little Girl', 'Dogs Are Everywhere' sympathized with the opposite sex through its disparaging observations of male behaviour. In *Record Mirror*, Jarvis talked of 'people who indulge in generally immoral behaviour, with no actual purpose. The way they shit on your carpet, that sort of thing. It's like low mindedness, brute instinct over higher values.' But in a 1995 interview with *Record Collector*, Jarvis was more specific.

' "Dogs Are Everywhere" was inspired one night after playing in Chesterfield. Magnus and Pete were always pissing about and getting stoned. Myself and Russell were puritanical and thought that was terrible. They'd have these mates hanging around, which got on my nerves. That night, they nicked bottles of beer from

Pete Mansell finally shows his face, only for Magnus Doyle to disappear.
Pulp and Fire chose this mannequin-ed photo as an official publicity shot
(*Karl Lang*)

behind the bar, and we got into loads of trouble. That's what "Dogs Are Everywhere" is about – people who display a doggish attitude.'

In case anyone thought Jarvis was preaching from his pulp-it by singing '*they always wag their tail at all the pretty girls and older women*', he also observes '*sometimes I have to wonder about the dog in me*.' The last thing he wanted to be was a preacher. 'We don't consciously think of ourselves as having this important thing to say, the "this is what I think" type of thing,' he told me in 1986. 'In many ways, I don't believe in coming out with big statements, like I'm some kind of spectator, looking at the world and moralizing and pontificating, like "this is what you should be". I would just hope that we don't *contribute* to the problem.'

The B-sides to 'Dogs' maintained the tension. 'Mark Of The

Devil' was Pulp's original choice for the A-side as they considered it their best song, though Jarvis felt the recorded version wasn't up to scratch. The mirth begins with: '*The mark of the devil is upon you; your look is no happier than mine/damnation is waiting in the mirror but you shouldn't mind.*' Jarvis then informed his anonymous correspondent, colourfully, that '*your past is just a bedroom full of implements of cruelty*'.

Violins to the fore, the track marked a new Eastern European folk tinge (think Slavs, gypsies and *Fiddler On The Roof*), betraying the mark of Russell, with a strange Eurodisco slant, but it seemed to fit Pulp's character. Like the blues, most folk music possesses an undertow of sadness as well as an invigorating air of community, born of hardship as well as celebration.

The second B-side, '97 Lovers' ('just take a short walk around town and you soon lose count of the deformities' read the sleeve) was another dark, slow melody that presented the first sign of Jarvis' fascination with domestic detail and sexual minutiae – '*I know a woman with a picture of Roger Moore in a short towelling dressing gown pinned to her bedroom wall/She married a man who works on a building site, now they make love beneath Roger every Friday night.*'

'It was the first time I got some good lyrics out,' he reckoned. The woman in question was his aunt. 'I always thought, God, it's weird that they're in bed having it off underneath that picture. My uncle must know she's probably thinking it's Roger whilst he's doing it to her.'

'Aborigine' was 'a real kitchen sink drama'. It got its title because Jarvis thought the primitive beat and bass notes on the violin sounded, yes, Aboriginal. The lyrical home truths, though, were universal: '*She wants excitement and she needs romance, all she gets is dirty underpants.*'

'Goodnight' – 'A concept piece that sounded like falling asleep,' according to Jarvis – was a sloowww, claustrophobic ballad, a story of wandering home, drunk and paranoid, that builds to a nightmare climax – '*When you awoke later that night, the bedroom was cold and you were alone/alone and afraid of the dark, watching, waiting, as you lie on your back, naked beneath the cold sheets; not dead, just sleeping.*'

The *Dogs EP* was an extreme-sounding record, well out of step with the trendier groups of the time, but the reviews were still positive. *Melody Maker* even gave Pulp their first Single Of The Week. 'Once you've heard Pulp, you'll never need The Smiths again,' it wildly claimed. 'Pulp are probably the most subversive, important band in the world today and they don't even know it.' Another *Melody Maker* journalist called them 'a thing of wild mis-shapen beauty'. One of Russell's regular missives to Fire announced that a French DJ in Serbo-Croatia thought Pulp 'his cup of tea'.

Despite torchbearers in the music press, none of the writers were influential enough to convert their peers, a necessary condition if Pulp were going to get the push as a Next Big Thing. The group did make the front cover of *Underground*, a new monthly magazine devoted to the consolidating indie culture, but Single Of The Week or not, 'Dogs Are Everywhere' unbelievably sold a miserable 300 copies. Maybe Pulp had to play live to be really appreciated, as Tony Perrin has said. Maybe this was music more at home in a 1930s Berlin nightclub than on a rock stage, where the new indie-pop was shaping up. Maybe people didn't like to have their noses rubbed in the facts of life in the way Pulp intended. Why bother, when you could have the more danceable dynamics of The Smiths and New Order, a much more listenable form of melancholy?

Both the above Mancunian groups had made an indelible mark on the 80s but The Smiths had been more influential as the decade progressed. Short, sharp, 60s-style melodies and guitars were everywhere, though the scene that was christened 'C86' (after a cassette of Brit-pop released in 1986 by the *NME*) had little of The Smiths' true class and much less of the group's iconoclastic verve.

Mirror on the wall, who are the freakiest of them all?
This became the cover of the *Dogs Are Everywhere EP*
(David Bocking)

But even in the era of The Wedding Present, The Shop Assistants and The Bodines, Pulp were renegades, quirks without the necessary 'cool' of the day. If passionate Euro-torchsong melancholy was cool, it was dressed in a charcoal-grey suit under a mop of greased hair and went by the name of Nick Cave, The Birthday Party's now solo vocalist. Even Scott Walker's 1983 comeback LP *Climate Of Hunter*, though massively acclaimed by the press, remains one of Virgin Records' worst-ever sellers on record.

Not that Pulp were ready to compromise in any way. 'Sometimes people get a bit annoyed and think we're wilfully not doing one thing or the other,' Jarvis told me in 1986. 'They think we change too much, which I can't see – but then I wouldn't. Maybe I'm just too crazy and confused. But I'd rather come across that way than have a normal rock approach – it's just a different way of getting through to people. If everybody does the same thing, it's such a cliché, and people don't listen to what you're saying any more, so you have to put things in a different way for them to listen.'

Russell was in full support: 'Some songs are more fragile than the rest – we can easily look stupid doing them. But they're usually the most rewarding when they go right. We'd rather fail miserably than just do all right.' As his standard letter accompanying Pulp's demos made clear. 'We don't fit into any particular musical category – all great artists set their own boundaries.' Sadly, audiences and tastemongers set theirs too, and Pulp were getting the cold shoulder.

As Jarvis was to discover, people would more readily listen to tales of woe and fumbling if interspersed with alleviating humour, as Morrissey and The Smiths were doing. Pulp were musically and lyrically heavy-browed, though Jarvis argued that the big-ballad form was meant to be ironic. 'A lot of our recent songs are more mock-dramatic,' he told me in 1986. 'I've got a thing at the moment about the fact that most things that you would expect to be quite dramatic, never turn out to be. You expect violins to come in at big dramatic points in your life when something happens, like my accident, but it never did. It was pathetic really. You're spoilt by watching films from an early age.

'It's funny, because you wouldn't think the music would turn out like it does when you think of the people involved in Pulp. Perhaps it's all a big accident. But it just seems a pretty good way of putting things across rather than us acting awkward. This type of music is almost a parody. It's not taken very seriously because it's seen as a bit of a Radio 2 thing, for middle-aged housewives, and not as art. But I think there's a lot more art to melodicism than that. People think of some of Burt Bacharach's songs as jolly MOR but some can really affect you, even if you think the lyrics or the person singing them are absolutely crap, like Tom Jones or somebody stupid, and there's nothing you can do about it. We're trying to use that but consciously, in a pure way, rather than those people who were Tin Pan Alley types writing hit-factory style. It's funny because they were also pulling people's heartstrings and yet they weren't bothered about it.'

Pulp were getting rather bitter and twisted, almost despising their peers. In a letter to Fire, Russell claimed that the band's interview technique needed discussing as 'Sadly, I think we're pretty boring to interview.' On the contrary, the boys were engrossingly quotable. In a memorable interview with *Zigzag* magazine Jarvis and Russell spelt out their grievances.

Target number one was punk, a movement which 'had disappeared up its own arse. Jaded cynics peddling pessimism – violent hardcore, pretentious spiky Batcave [referring to the goth movement], new age hippie punk. It was a multi-coloured refraction of the white light.' *POW!*

'Outside,' they claimed, 'it was all happy-happy bubblegum. Thrusting crotches in the race to become the Mike Yarwood of pop. New technocrats selling sex to teenagers, fiddling around with knobs and rooting around the past as if it were a jumble sale.' *OOF!*

Not only that but 'social conscience music had a nauseating effect'. Nena, the German singer behind the fluffy singalong but clearly anti-nuclear number one '99 Luftballons', 'makes millions of out nuclear fears and takes the edge off people's anger, diffusing any pressure for change.' *KAPOW!*

As Jarvis concluded, 'Our chosen means of expression was populated by diluters and devaluers of music that once meant something.' *BOFFO!*

In other words, Jarvis wasn't quite the flippant rake and endearing raconteur we know and love today. His current relationship was failing, Pulp was stalling, and even though he had had his first taste of freedom by leaving home, he had shifted into an old warehouse (known as The Wicker) full of Sheffield oddities, as well as rival model railway enthusiasts (Jarvis remembers that they used to crap outside each other's front door), a table tennis club and rehearsal space for bands. Jarvis was well into his jumble-sale phase by now, but he admitted it was a habit that had got out of hand; he practically filled up his room with bags of clothes, clearly stress-related, obsessive behaviour.

In 1994, Fire asked Jarvis to write some sleevenotes for *Masters Of The Universe*, a compilation of Pulp's early EPs. He wrote, 'These songs stem from probably the most depressing period in my life (bar nine months I spent living in a tower block in Mile End in 1989) and I guess this is reflected in the music and lyrics. I think we were all frustrated and angry in some way and you can hear that tension. They were recorded in Sheffield in crappy little studios for hardly any money – oh yes, you know the score, but despite all that I think there is still a spirit that comes through them. Listening to those tracks again after all this time was quite an experience – I felt by turns excited, surprised, embarrassed, sad and proud. At least we were striving for something, reaching for something we couldn't attain, but trying all the same.'

Jealousy must have compounded their gloomy worldview. Russell: 'It all obviously resulted in a certain amount of bitterness when you see cacky bands zooming past you, like lesser watered-down versions of a small facet of what you were doing. They'd romp past and you'd be thinking "What the fuck is this?", but we always thought we were good and that's why we stuck at it. We lived very frugally during those times.' But as he later admitted, driven by the ambition to make 'the best music in the world, out of necessity, you think what others are trying to do is not so good, so in a way, you have to hate other bands.'

It was hard for Jarvis to accept The Smiths' success. The Mancunians had released their first record the same year as Pulp 'and had a rather larger impact,' Jarvis noted, acidly. 'Yes, I was jealous of *him*, because they were from the North and in a faintly similar vein to us, compared to everything else around. But I resented anyone who was successful.'

Was it professional jealousy that makes Jarvis say he has never liked The Smiths anyway? 'I thought Morrissey's words were all right sometimes, and I liked a couple of songs, like "Girlfriend In A Coma", but it all didn't have much of a tune to it for me, and I just don't think he can sing, which is his problem, I'd say,' is his argument. 'And I've never been into this "Johnny Marr, guitarist for a generation" stuff.'

Fair enough. But Pulp weren't even that happy amongst themselves. 'We don't hang around with each other: we don't like each other very much,' he admitted then. 'There is a certain tension – I don't like it when everyone gets comfortable.'

'I'm a bit of a dictator sometimes,' he told *Melody Maker*. 'I surprise myself because I can be a bit obnoxious. I think it's because it means a lot to me. I can be a bit of a twat sometimes. In concerts I stop songs half way through. I know it's not a good thing to do but I can't help myself. I'm going to have to go and see my analyst.'

5

out come the freaks

By the time Pulp had signed to Fire, Tony Perrin had stopped managing their affairs. He was about to take on The Mission (formed by ex-Sisters Of Mercy guitarist Wayne Hussey, with Simon Hinkler on board) but Perrin had already decided he'd gone as far as he could with Pulp. 'I could appreciate they weren't happy with *It* but I wasn't really confident of where they appeared to be going. We were going in different directions and I couldn't do anything for them.'

Russell took over the business side, hustling for shows, press and radio promotion and hustling Fire, but Pulp lost a manager's invaluable role as a go-between, and found itself at the mercy of the often fragile relationship between an independent label and group where both live hand to mouth, sometimes from week to week, especially in the hard-up 80s.

When it came to Pulp recording a full-length album, Fire could only afford £600, which provided just a week of recording and mixing, without the option of a real producer to guide them (the producer employed subsequently asked to be left off the credits!). In his defence, Clive Solomon said that Pulp got the studio they requested, and that 'they weren't into making polished sounding records at that time. Everyone was pleasant and courteous, and nobody complained.'

The album sessions took place in June, at Input Studios in Sheffield. 'Don't You Know' was the first track to emerge, on a vinyl compilation album *Fruitcakes And Fur Collars*, given away with *Record Mirror* on 27 September, followed a month later by a two-track single on Fire.

The A-side was 'They Suffocate At Night', a beautiful if chilling ballad. Take it away, Jarvis: *'Festering in silence, growing in the dark, and this they saw as love, love, so sad to see; they suffocate at night . . .'*

The B-side, 'Tunnel', was the lengthy, allegorical tale of losing direction that Jarvis referred to in his sleevenotes to *Masters Of The Universe*, though there was an underlying theme of staying alive by searching for the tunnel's exit. The single won ambivalent reviews this time (maybe Pulp's loyal scribes had to let someone else write about them). 'Very nice,' said *NME*. 'Not, however, terribly interesting, being a croon through softly singing electric guitars with a fairly feeble melody and a voice with a frog in its throat. Could try harder.'

The band made a video for 'They Suffocate at Night', though it didn't make any difference. No wonder, really, as Jarvis explains: 'It was made by someone who claimed to have done the lighting on *Chariots Of Fire*, which impressed us a great deal at the time. In typical Fire fashion, we could only afford one roll of film, so he had to keep winding the film backwards and forwards for different bits of the song. I converted an inspection pit, in an abandoned warehouse across the road from the factory where I was living, into a sunken bedroom and then filled 200 freezer bags full of coloured liquid for another bit of a set elsewhere. For some reason, there was a horse skeleton in the building so that ended up in the film too. I remember being quite pleased with it at the time. My sister Saskia and a friend, Steve Genn, played two lovers and we kind of watched. The filming went on till four o'clock in the morning and at the end of it, the band split. What a great evening.'

The internal tension that inspired 'Dogs Are Everywhere' had finally come to a head. Russell: 'Jarvis and I were always seriously committed while Magnus and Pete just wanted to have a laugh, with Candida a bit ambivalent in between. It was my fault really, with hindsight. Now I wouldn't be so judgemental about them having a laugh because I'm probably more like that myself now, but back then, the band was like the air we breathed, and I was trying to run things like a well oiled military machine. The video shoot was costing several hundreds of pounds, and it was late, and wet, and they were pissed, and pissing about, so they got the boot.'

Candida: 'Russell was quite different then. He'd be really cross when we'd turn up late for practices and that we wouldn't really put as much into it as they did although they never particularly demanded us to. But that's where the clashes came.' As Magnus' sister and Peter's girlfriend, she had little choice over which side to take, and so left in sympathy.

By all accounts, Peter could be a stroppy, opinionated character, but Magnus was more volatile and unpredictable. 'You could write a book just about Magnus,' Tony Perrin reckons. My fondest memory of him was in Holland, when he dressed in a monk's habit, head shaved, blessing people. He was probably the maddest person I'd ever met, but an absolutely magnificent character with it, just with a different logic and set of values to the rest of us. Like Keith Moon, when he played, he became part of the kit.'

At one show, Magnus threw his kit to the floor after each song, forcing the band to reassemble it before the next. 'He was always wild,' Candida sighs. 'But he was a brilliant drummer. He could have had such a career but he wasn't interested, even after Pulp. He got right into the hallucinogenic drug scene, and he was always someone who'd have to take loads more than anyone else. He just didn't fit into Sheffield after that, and got quite into religion. Last I heard, he'd changed his name. He's been in India for eighteen months, and no one's heard from him. I don't think he's dead or anything but it must be pretty bad for my parents.'

So exit three Pulps, and enter drummer Nick Banks, an ex-member of groups like God, The Vicious Circles and Phono Industria. More importantly, he was the nephew of English soccer's most famous goalie, Gordon Banks.

Of stocky build, with a more down-to-earth, pragmatic nature than the usual Pulp misfit, Nick had first seen the group play in 1982, at the end of his sixth-form year. 'I was blown away as they were so completely different, on this big stage with all these paper fish everywhere, and these really lush songs. I did a stint promoting bands at the Hallamshire, including Pulp and various Pulp offshoot bands. When Magnus and Pete were leaving, I was playing in various groups but I saw an ad for a drummer, knew Jarvis to speak to, and asked him to give me a go.'

When Nick went to Jarvis' house for the audition, he was followed all the way from the bus stop by an English bull terrier which they had to get rid of because Jarvis' family dog was going spare. As Jarvis recalls, 'We'd kick it onto the main road, and hope it would lead us back to the owner. The police station was shut, so we put it in a garden with a fence. During the course of walking around, we talked and got on well, so we thought we'd have him. We'd never heard him play drums and certainly wouldn't have if we had.'

Having been out of the band for several months, Candida had also seen an ad for her replacement, specifically asking for a female keyboardist. 'I thought, "Bastards, that's a bit nasty." But they must have rung me up a bit later and asked me back, as I went along for a practice. Pete was going to rejoin as well but Magnus wouldn't go along, though we tried convincing him. Actually, he did turn up once but Nick was there, drumming, which made a weird atmosphere. But I'm glad I went back.'

Russell: 'I don't know why Candida stuck it so long but I'm glad she has. If she ever left, a certain part of the soul of the band would go too. For one, she's a woman, which stops us getting too crude about things, and in her own way, she's quite hardline and strong, with a certain style about her, like a girl/woman. Between Pulp duties, her job was working in toy shops, which fitted her well as she's always collecting little plastic rings and cracker novelties and stuff. The reason our music's been original is because of

Spring is in the air . . . Jarvis in London, 1986
(Meir Gal)

a clash of five disparate personalities, who probably abhorred each other's way of living but had a mutual love of things, like going around second-hand shops and making the music we did.'

The 'second-hand' fetish was definitely part of Pulp's soul. It manifested itself in clothes and in the love of 'gew-gaw' – a Victorian word meaning oddments, bits and bobs, according to Russell. 'In a way we were very conservative, with a small 'c'. You'd see video game rooms where there used to be a sarsaparilla bar, but we were battling for the sarsaparilla bar and other funny little things that used to exist in the past.'

Later on, Jarvis would lament the passing of crucial items like metal lids on Marmite, Cresta drinks (*'it's frothy maan!'* as the ad went) and Spangles. What is it about Northerners and their lamenting of the good old days? 'In our way,' Russell contends, 'we clung on to odd little Northern things because they felt more

No escaping those fishes . . . Jarvis in London again
(Meir Gal)

real and more tactile, with some atmosphere to them. Somebody once described Sheffield as the Northern Twin Peaks, which I thought was quite astute 'cos that's what a lot of the songs are about, and part of the atmosphere of the music is the seediness underneath it all. Maybe it doesn't *really* have that, but all other cities have been in a spotlight – you know what a Scouser's like as you can see them on *Brookside* – whereas Sheffield has its own culture that has never been subject to inspection.'

By this point, Pulp were probably feeling second-hand too. It made commercial sense to pre-empt the forthcoming album with a single but time rolled on again, with no release date in sight. It seemed that Fire were having financial problems – the main reason for the album's delay was that Input Studios were holding on to the master tapes until Fire paid for them.

The album finally saw the light of day in May of 1987, nearly a year after it was finished. Titled *Freaks*, it had the telling subtitle 'ten stories about power, claustrophobia, suffocation and holding hands'. Even more telling, the cover was a distorted, hall-of-mirrors portrait of Pulp.

'These freaks we're talking about, they're formal people gone a bit wrong, that's all,' the brief sleevenotes explained. 'Something happened to them and they never got over it. Now they walk around with twisted innards and blank faces, wanting to join in but too scared to make the jump. It's sad but don't bother crying: they still eat and drink and watch TV just like everybody else. And they smoke.'

'Either the songs are freaks or the people in them are,' Jarvis explained, 'but it's not a concept record.' Yet the songs, he admitted, were inspired by the disintegrating relationship with his first girlfriend. 'The freaks thing is like getting divorced from the rest of the world by something like that relationship,' he mused.

Worse, 'I felt like I was turning into a freak myself.' His experiences living in the warehouse – 'a drop-in centre for all the freaks and misfits of Sheffield' – was obviously getting to him too, and alienation from his surroundings was becoming almost total. 'We'd been doing something worthwhile and original and yet nobody seemed interested,' he moaned. 'It was the dark days of the 80s, the "we're heading for a boom time, let's be happy attitude".'

References in the press to looking like freaks didn't help either. *Sounds* had famously described Pulp as 'the escape party from *One Flew Over The Cuckoo's Nest*', words meant affectionately but which Jarvis felt were too predictable. 'When we play live,' he told *Sounds*, 'everyone dwells on the fact I'm thin with specs, Russell looks like Count Dracula, Candida, although she's twenty-three, looks fourteen while Pete looks like a football hooligan. We were always getting called freaks so we thought, let's call the LP *Freaks* just to . . . put two fingers up.' Hence *Freaks* was a title both serious and a way to send themselves up.

Russell likened *Freaks* to the works of British psychosexual-specializing author Ian McEwan, calling it 'claustrophobic and obsessive and clammy'. If Pulp had turned the art of the 'house-wife's choice' ballad on its head, as if Scott Walker were signing on the dole in Sheffield, then the listener needed a housewife's dose of Valium to get through the album. From its opening words – *'Sometimes, nature makes mistakes,'* delivered by Russell in that unfettered Yorkshire accent – *Freaks* was heavy going, but still a *tour-de-force* that stands up to the test of time.

'Fairground' was an uptempo, frenetic opener, out of line with the rest of the album, but its parade of nature's mistakes sets the tone. The haunted arrangement and disturbing lyric mirrored the atmosphere of Tod Browning's 1932 film classic *Freaks*, where the twin reactions of cruel laughter and shrinking fear that fairground freaks elicit battle it out.

Jarvis' mesmeric tragi-balladry took over from here, through 'I Want You' (*'I'll throw myself away, I'll break you because I love myself in you'*), 'Being Followed Home' (fear and loathing in Sheffield where *'the street stinks of piss and dead fish'*), 'Life Must Be So Wonderful' (*'Now all our dreams melt in the sun and visions dwindle one by one'*), 'There's No Emotion' (*'In your heart, there's no emotion and your soul, your soul just dried away. There's no love, no love left in your body'*) and 'They Suffocate At Night' (*'Two years have passed, two years of emptiness inside'*).

There were odd breaks to the lovelorn formula. 'Master Of The Universe' was a jerky throttler with an Eastern European undertow and words that suggested Jarvis was battling with his ego (though the song got its name from some shampoo he'd bought after recovering from his accident, at a time when Jarvis probably felt like master of none). 'Anorexic Beauty' was a real oddity, jerky and reserved, with Russell singing words written by David Kurley from New Model Soldier, Magnus on guitar and Jarvis on drums. The noisy, staccato 'Never-Ending Story' detailed the ease by which you can restart a relationship you know is doomed. Then there was 'Don't You Know', by comparison outrageously carefree and poppy, and a hint of what was to come in the 90s. Not that Jarvis was feeling happy or anything: *'So just lie back and enjoy it and save your tears for when the kissing stops, oh you know it's got to stop.'*

In Jarvis' mind, the problem was that, 'people identify optimism with false jollity, and rebelling against that makes you seem pessimistic and nihilistic. But we're ten years on from all that, so it's time for something more simplified, which is why the music of *Freaks* is about seeing a kind of irony.'

That may be so, but *Freak*'s unrelenting effect was so bleak and draining that the only irony was how seductive misery could sound. The album was certainly uncontaminated by humour (the background guffaws in 'Fairground' were more the sound of asylum inmates). Between the innocence of *It* and the cynicism of alienation, Pulp had lost sight of the middle ground – and created a masterpiece of sorts in the process.

NME might have remained indifferent to Pulp's charms but *Melody Maker* was supportive and *Sounds* nearly hyperventilating: '*Freaks* turned the conveyance of moroseness into a fine art. They do it with style, cleverly ill-defined wit and even charm, softening us up with chirpy organ fizz-bangs and swooping violins; and then they make their move, charging forward with lyrical cut-lasses flailing in all directions. We are left in a damaged condition, ripped and torn and literally drained of all optimism . . . a jagged collection of cruel words fastened to frequently enthralling music.'

Jarvis felt *Freaks* contained some good songs but was badly let down by its production. It transpired that they had done a rough mix, but when they returned to the studio, they discovered that the owner had scrubbed the master tapes to use for another recording. Pulp had no choice but to go with the rough mix. When the album was well received, the group seemed happy enough, but months later, when they were in the process of leaving Fire, they heavily panned it. Russell maintained that the budget they were operating under meant 'all you can communicate is darkness, and scratch away and be really intense. You can't have really big, lush sounds.' But wasn't that what Pulp wanted, after the lushness of *It*?

At least the reviews were now taking them seriously. 'Pulp are creating a music that is virtually without peer in the Britain of 1987,' was *Sounds'* tack in an interview feature, which also placed them in the context of Ian McEwan, pre-war German dramatist/composer Bertolt Brecht and, er, *Carry On* comedian Charles Hawtrey. The group moaned again. 'They make us seem a bit contrived when, hopefully, it's quite raw, getting at emotional nerve endings,' said Jarvis. Yet they seemed to enjoy talking about trivia, like Jarvis and Russell's love of *The Antiques Roadshow* – Jarvis specialized in 50s art deco, Russell in Italian seventeenth-century painting. But Jarvis was serious too, admitting he was never a carefree adolescent. 'I wouldn't go out with me if I were you,' he said, glumly.

A year after *Freaks* had been written, I asked Jarvis if he had been in love again. 'I don't really like to use that word anymore,' he shrugged, without much obvious irony. 'I don't know what it's supposed to mean.'

6

my grandmother's legendary keyboard

In 1985, Jarvis reckoned being stuck in a wheelchair on stage had been a disadvantage 'but it made me move my head more. That's probably what inspired our new Euro-disco direction.'

'Mark Of The Devil' aside, this sea-change was hardly evident but Jarvis had somehow decided disco was the way forward, 'because I was sick of the over-the-top emotional business. Giorgio Moroder didn't have any emotion: it was robot music. I was intrigued with the idea of that beat and style but with something emotional over the top.' The irony Pulp intended was too subtle – now it was time to be blatant.

Where else would the trigger come from for Pulp if not an unexpected, cheap source? Jarvis' grandma had recently bought a portable keyboard, with inbuilt rhythms, which suited his purposes. 'Because it made music without any feeling at all, because it was a machine, something about it appealed, so that was the turning point, and I started doing more disco things. So I nicked her keyboard. I've still got it actually. I think she gave up after a few days anyway, so I don't think she missed it too much.'

In 1987, Jarvis did a one-off concert at Sheffield Polytechnic with a certain Captain Sleep on the aforementioned Yamaha Portasound keyboard (Candida was still out of the band) and some self-confessed 'daft disco songs'. But the good Captain found it difficult staying awake for more than two hours, which Jarvis found too depressing, and he was dispensed with. Candida

Pulp number four, with Stephen Havenhand momentarily in the frame
(*David Bocking*)

subsequently returned, with Stephen Havenhand from Sheffield band Lay Of The Land momentarily joining on bass.

'Stephen was a good songwriter but the shyest person I've ever met,' Jarvis told *Record Collector*. 'He wouldn't loosen up so, in the end, he left. Plus you couldn't hear him play the bass – he was so gentle with the strings, like he didn't want to disturb!'

The rest of Pulp had mixed feelings about Jarvis' new direction. Russell saw it as a chance to be musically adventurous while Nick was already a dance music fan, and relished giving people the chance to dance 'should they wish to, rather than having weird stops and time changes and then a jazz bit or something.'

Candida felt differently. Despite her love of *Saturday Night Fever*, she wasn't keen. 'It was weird. The first new song was "She's A Lady", which reminded me of a song by Boney M, and it just didn't feel right playing it at all.Songs like "Death II" and "Countdown" were very different from the Pulp I'd been in before, and it was weird being there without Magnus and Pete to begin with.'

Fire, meanwhile, had filled the silence by releasing 'Master Of The Universe' as a single, though in its sanitized, radio-friendly version. At the time, Jarvis said he was unhappy at the decision. 'Our version is intensely embarassing,' he decided. 'My voice – I don't know what I was thinking of.'

Yet Clive Solomon cites this as an example of Pulp rewriting history. 'We didn't think "Master" was a strong single. It had a bit of a heavy metal edge, so we didn't expect people who liked Pulp to give it a good reaction. It was the band's decision.'

He quotes a letter from Jarvis to support his opinion. 'If you're worried about the words "masturbate" and "comes" in the lyric,' Jarvis wrote, 'there is a sanitized version which substitutes "vegetates" and "keeps" to keep the kiddies happy. We took a tape of the song down to The Limit and got a general thumbs up from DJs and clientele alike. So there you have it. I'm afraid we're fairly immovable on this one, lads, and I think you should respect our judgement. After all, I think the *Dogs Are Everywhere EP* would have done a lot better had "Mark Of The Devil" been the title track as we suggested at the time. Anyway, let us know what you think so we can get things moving.'

It was hard to deny that Solomon had a point, one which is backed up by Robin Gibson, a *Sounds* freelance writer who was helping out at Fire. 'Pulp were so proud of "Master Of The Universe",' he recalls. 'It was the same as with *Freaks*, which everyone thought very highly of at the time, but decided it was a load of shit later. But we would never release a record against a band's will.'

The two extra tracks weren't Pulp's best either. 'Manon' was an overdubbed version of a track from the *Freaks* sessions, where Jarvis' voice dangerously wavers and cracks. He admitted the track was a rip-off of Serge Gainsbourg, another intense Gallic balladeer, but more bawdy and commercial than Jacques Brel. 'Embarrassingly for me, I thought it was a man's name at the time, but I've since learnt that it's a woman's.'

As for the last track, 'Silence', plucked from a pre-'Little Girl' demo recorded in May 1984, it remains Jarvis' most hated Pulp track aired to the public – 'a two-note keyboard drone, someone playing one of those hunting horns you have on the living room wall and me alternately talking and screaming this story about a love affair that doesn't work out.' When Fire released the album *Masters Of The Universe* in 1994, Jarvis banned its inclusion: 'I couldn't live with it being out,' he exclaimed. Anyone listening to its tortured amateur dramaticism (Jarvis likens the bedroom to a funeral parlour) could only agree.

'Silence' may have been an old track but it seemed to represent a bridge too far. It was clearly time for a rethink. Anyway, Pulp had run out of songs, and weren't going to record any more for Fire, who were firmly in their bad books. 'After *Freaks*,' Clive Solomon cagily ventures, 'perhaps Pulp thought they weren't getting very far. I would have been happy to have carried on but they took a bit of time to find a company that could put more behind them.'

Having signed a short term agreement, Pulp were free to leave Fire, and subsequently fell in with Dave Taylor and his partner, ex-*NME* journalist Amrik Rai – 'A man associated with having his finger on the pulse,' according to Jarvis. Not that Jarvis was one to be concerned with fingers on pulses. According to Dave Bedford, who had taken over Johnny Waller's duties at Fire, 'They liked the idea of new technology and a comfy, new studio.'

Rai was certainly well-connected. He was managing Sheffield legends Cabaret Voltaire and Chakk, who were one of 1986's Next Big Things (they made the cover of *Melody Maker* with their first single, just like Suede). Chakk landed a sizeable deal with MCA and Rai suggested the group use the money to form a company, called FON (standing for 'Fuck Off Nazis'), and build a studio, which they did, just doors down from The Wicker abode and Pulp's rehearsal rooms. Taylor and Rai then looked to start a label, also called FON.

In a local fanzine, Taylor said, 'Pulp strike me as a really special band. They should have a higher profile because they deserve it.' To which Rai added, 'I'd be interested in Pulp if they could make a classic garage Scott Walker track.'

Russell, meanwhile praised the duo. 'FON have spent more money on pizzas than Fire ever did on promotion,' he claimed, basking in some financial flattery, and a marriage made in Sheffield heaven seemed on the cards.

In reality, Rai admits he didn't think that much of Pulp: 'Though Jarvis was always an interesting character. He used to hang out at Graves Coffee Bar at the university, because it was cheap. We'd all go to the student parties, as the scene centred around Psalter Lane Art College and the coffee bar, and everyone lived in the same area – in Broomehall, where they caught the Yorkshire Ripper. But Jarvis never fitted into that scene, which was very industrial-like, with bands like Hula and Clock DVA and the Cabs. There were arty bands like Artery but people saw Pulp as everyone's poor cousins. They'd say hello to Jarvis but not go as far as to buy him a drink. People thought he was pretty talented but also thought that his time would never come. Sheffield was quite a cool city, living as it did in the shadow of Manchester, with lots of pretentions, while Jarvis was a natural.'

Still, a FON release was planned and Pulp entered FON Studios in July of 1987 and recorded 'Don't You Want Me Anymore?' and 'Rattlesnake'. The latter was to be the new B-side to 'Death Comes To Town', recorded five months later alongside a disco-remix version, 'Death Goes To The Disco', with new bassist Anthony Genn (brother of Steve from Mr Morality and the 'They Suffocate At Night' video). Genn was a young, extrovert, exhibitionist of a character who sometimes ended up naked on stage. (He made music press headlines at 1995's Glastonbury festival when he streaked on stage during Elastica's set. He subsequently joined them on keyboards!)

The music may have been gloomy but Pulp were always game for a laugh on stage. On one occasion, Jarvis leapt into the air and his glasses flew off. He searched around the stage for them, eventually finding them in the drum riser. Equally in character was the time Russell, furious over an argument about money after a show at the Leadmill, promptly took his frustrations out on the dressing room. The next morning, he was seen sneaking back in with replacement lightbulbs . . .

As with 'Maureen' (the track was only ever released on a cassette magazine *Premspeak 1*, released by a member of Dig Vis Drill), Pulp made a video for 'Death Comes To Town' without having a release date for the single. Besides some film Jarvis had shot at a fairground, plus footage hijacked from National Geographic videos, the bulk of the action came from a one-off Leadmill show on 9 August 1987. The so-called 'The Day That Never Happened' show meant special decorations – silver foil mobiles, bags of coloured water hanging off white-sprayed trees, super-8 and slide films, and, to top it all, snowfall blown across the stage by hair-dryers. The usual stuff, then. 'A cosmic tangerine experience,' was Russell's opinion, but it was generally believed to have been a bit of a shaky affair, the work of The Crimplene Underground.

And then days turned into weeks into months.

Jarvis: 'The stuff we did at FON was our best recordings ever, done in a proper studio with as much time as we needed, and a string section. Then FON decided not to release them.' The delay was nothing new to our star-in-waiting. 'That's just the way my life is meant to go,' he later concluded. 'At a snail's pace with time to reflect on the horror of life in between.'

FON never did release a Pulp record. After the Fire frustrations, the band had jumped out of the frying pan into, yes, another fire. Did FON lose interest because Pulp were abandoning the 'garage Scott Walker' schtick for 'disco Scott Walker'? Future Pulp bassist Steve Mackey reckoned FON had done the same to several groups. 'The label's only real success was with Age Of Chance's cover of Prince's "Kiss" – and Rai agrees that the problem wasn't personal but down to in-fighting between members of Chakk.'

'I got fed up and decided I didn't want any more to do with it,' Rai admits. 'Anyway, it was all a bit low-key around Pulp as no one believed they would break. There was a general air of disillusionment in Sheffield all around then. It was great when nothing was going on, because when it did, there was so much backbiting going around. It was the fourth or fifth biggest city in the UK, which should have had a much bigger scene, as Martin Fry or Phil Oakey would tell people too. But after ABC and The Human League's success, no one was encouraged to do anything, unlike in Manchester, where they're all scam merchants and jump on board and ride it till the cows come home! Maybe Sheffield was like a socialist republic of South Yorkshire, where they'd rather everyone was doing nothing at all.'

Jarvis must also have sensed the encroaching ennui as he had already decided not to stick around. He'd been attending a one-day film course at Sheffield Poly but the rest of the time, he and the band were stuck in a living limbo. 'You used to see them in either the Washington or the Hallamshire, which is where musicians tended to go, and they used to sit in the corner, always the same table, always with the same crowd,' recalls fellow Poly student Rob Jefferson.

Jarvis had even lost his place at Liverpool University because he'd deferred entrance so many times. But despite his apathy, he managed to get it together to apply to London's prestigious St Martin's School Of Art to do a degree in film, and because of a general artistic bent and vital video/film experience, he was accepted. Say hello to Sheffield, wave goodbye . . .

'I had to realize I'd taken a wrong turn,' he told *Select* in 1995. 'You know when you're in a car and you take a wrong turn, you don't like to admit it, do you? You think if you keep going you'll come right again. But you don't, do you? I'd spent the best part of a decade in bed and in an unsuccessful band. I was forced to admit I'd been wasting my time. But I was lucky enough to get into St Martin's, so I was off. I just imagined the group would cease to exist.'

The rest of Pulp were left to their own devices. Russell's interest in antiques had developed into a business (mostly glassware) and he had started drawing up the origins of a board game, The Housing Ladder (based on the housing market). He was settled in Sheffield, with his girlfriend, who was soon to give birth to a daughter (they now have two children). Candida ruefully returned to the dole but soon moved to Manchester and started working in a toy shop while Nick was gainfully employed in a number of jobs – wreath-making and teaching design technology being two – together with spells on the dole, living in both London and Sheffield.

Anthony Genn had less luck. Another unpredictable character

like Magnus Doyle, a penchant for acid caused him to, as Jarvis saw it, 'flip out'. Rob Mitchell remembers hearing him say, '"acid is the only reality", and the next thing, he'd joined the church.'

But not just any old church. No, it was the now infamous 'Nine O'Clock Service' collective in Sheffield led by 'rave vicar' Chris Brain which made national news in October 1994 for sex-scandal revelations and brainwashing disciples with breakbeats. Sheffield really *was* Sex City. The same church, in fact, that ex-Pulp member Peter Dalton had also ended up joining in 1986 (high up in the ranks too, just below Chris Brain). What *was* it with these Pulp people?

According to one of Genn's best friends, Steve Mackey, who was to replace him on bass, 'The acid fucked Anthony's life up and he started owing lots of money to different places. Then an envelope came through his door containing £760, which was curiously the exact amount of money he needed to pay off his bills, followed by a visit from these twelve Christians later that night, who sat around and talked through his problems, and said they could help if he came into the church. That's how they used to work. He left after three years, saying it was fucking weird, that they were all shagging each other and "you won't believe what's going on there." We thought he was being a bit fucked up so when it all came out in the news, lots of people were doing lots of apologizing to him.'

If Jarvis once claimed that Pulp's fans were 'mentally unbalanced', what about the members? *One Flew Over The Cuckoo's Nest* was right. 'If I didn't get out of Sheffield sharpish,' Jarvis realized, 'I was going to end up as a sad character who used to be in a band.'

7

down and up and out in london

After six years, Jarvis finally went to college. He'd followed one individual muse, and now it was time to follow another: he'd enjoyed making films at school, so here was a chance to get away from Sheffield and music and into something new, creative and open-ended. Phew.

The first task was to find somewhere to live. Jarvis wasn't known for his organizational abilities so let's be grateful that, at this juncture, Steve Mackey entered his life on a full-time basis.

Once a member of snappily named MC5/Stooges-style metal/punksters Trolley Dog Shag, the tall, boyishly handsome Mackey had cut his shaggy hair and come to London to study film production at Goldsmiths College, while working part-time as a runner on commercials and pop videos.

He'd known Jarvis for years. 'Me and Steve Genn used to get really stoned, and on Friday nights, we'd go to the pub in Sheffield with the express intention to get Jarvis to tell us some stories. For an hour and a half, he'd just talk about anything, and we'd sit there laughing, slightly at him and slightly with him, which he didn't mind that much! I used to go and watch Pulp, as everyone did in Sheffield. They were an institution because they had an intensity that nobody else had, which really stood out. Speaking from hindsight, there was absolutely no inclination then that Pulp might make it and Jarvis might be a star because there was the C86 movement, then House music, then Shoegazing. It was like, "the world is wrong and Jarvis is right".'

As Steve subsequently discovered: 'Jarvis didn't have anywhere to live but I'd found out there was another squat the floor above where I was squatting in Camberwell, on the fourteenth floor.' Camberwell was a popular low-rent suburb, dotted with council estates and imposing Georgian mansions. It wasn't deadsville but neither was it salubrious.

'I said I'd sell him my squat for £150, the reason being it was a really torrid block, with kids shooting up on the stairs, so I'd paid for one of those metal doors to be put on which meant no one could break in. So Jarvis and his friend Martin moved in and we moved in upstairs, because the view from there faced the whole of London as opposed to just Brixton. I felt bad about asking for money but my flatmate, who was a merchant banker who earned £40,000 a year, was quite hardnosed. Jarvis moved in and then asked if I wanted to be in Pulp. I said, "yeah" just like that. I knew Pulp hadn't been successful but, coming from Sheffield, you knew that they were real and genuine. They were a small legend there – 1000 people would go to see them.'

Jarvis wasn't prepared to let Pulp disappear, and he saw Steve's joining as one way to stop them splitting up. Instead, the group entered a period of semi-hibernation, meeting on a bi-monthly basis, playing odd shows but avoiding any concrete plans (without a record deal or money, what could they do?). Eighteen months lay between their last session at FON and Pulp's eventual return to the studio, which gave Jarvis time to concentrate on studies and acclimatize himself to London.

The experience was initially grim: the Camberwell squat wasn't exactly rent-a-home-sweet-home, and when he shifted to a tower block in the East End deadzone of Mile End, matters got even worse (he ended up returning to Camberwell). Jarvis admits it took him those eighteen months to start feeling at all settled. 'It would have been easier to stay in Sheffield – I knew lots of people and felt I had the measure of the place, and then you come to London. In Sheffield, everyone congregates in the centre of town

Pulp as we know them today, with new member Steve Mackey on board. Jarvis meanwhile, gets to grip with contact lenses
(Alistair Indge)

at weekends, which of course they don't do in London, so I'd do sad things like ending up walking around Piccadilly Circus on a Saturday night, wondering where everybody was, but of course it's all tourists. It takes a bit of time to learn these things, and the fact you have to be quite organized about your social life, and meeting people at a certain time and a certain place, because there were only ever two pubs in Sheffield that people went to. You'd walk around London for two months expecting to bump into someone and never did.'

Despite being wary of believing in myths over reality, Jarvis was led by his naivety. 'I'd heard about St Martin's, read about it in books, and thought this is going to be the glamour I've been looking for, there in the capital city; it will occur. Of course it didn't.' Worse, he failed to score on the female front for the first two years after he moved to London. 'Lover's block,' he called it. London was an anonymous city, and he was no go-getter. 'It makes you appreciate it when you finally get around to doing it,' he underlines.

As a cutting-edge art institution, St Martin's was a minefield of ambitions and pretensions, which presented a challenge for the still-provincial Jarv. 'What they tried to do on our course was a very clear example of right-on-ness. They basically had a Noah's Ark of every ethnic and sexual persuasion that they could – there were two gays, two black people, a Chinese, a couple of Germans, and me and this kid from Liverpool were the token Northerners. The next year, we got a disabled person in, as they probably thought there was something missing.'

Welcome to Mis-shapes Central. 'It was done for some daft *Guardian*-reader reason but it was probably the best thing they could have done because it was very interesting to be among people who were completely different to yourself. I found that exciting.'

Even more exciting was the Acid House explosion sweeping through London and Manchester. Jarvis and Steve embraced the brave new world by attending the giant raves held in and around the M25 orbital region. After years of diligent outsidership, this was Jarvis' first experience of community sharing as well as seratonin-enhancing drugs. 'Basically, I became a drug addict. I surprised myself by how much I got into it. I'd never been particularly into trends before.'

Steve Mackey: ' "Sorted For E's And Wizz" totally sums up that whole period. I was then living with Barbara Ellen, an *NME* journalist, and we'd started going to Phuture, which was the first Balearic club. My role in Pulp then was the modernizer, as I was really into Acid and House music, and while Jarvis converted me to Scott Walker and Serge Gainsbourg, I got Jarvis into House. So we'd all go to raves like Sunrise and Biology, every weekend, and take drugs, as everyone did, and we became obsessed with technology. We really thought our lives were changing, and the whole world around us. As outsiders, the community atmosphere was quite a special thing.'

From fairground freaks to fairground rides, in just over a year! It's amazing what drugs can do. 'Plus it was at the end of the 80s, a really bad time for us as nothing good had happened, we couldn't believe The Smiths were successful because Morrissey's got such an awful voice and just repeated the same thing over and over, ad nauseam, and then all this music came along which sounded like the music from the future, like *Star Trek*. You'd go to these raves and it was like a spaceship had landed! Lights were flashing, there were sexy girls, the music was like Kraftwerk . . . It was like the future and you were part of it, and for a while, it was like a little secret. Then record companies got involved and it went commercial, but there was a moment when the songs and the movement were bigger than everything else. We used to be gobsmacked . . . you'd go home every day and put on things like Derrick May's "Strings Of Life" and "Someday" by C.C. Rodgers, so many great songs.'

With such distractions, Pulp were never going to get organized. They were only playing odd shows, such as the concert at Sheffield Limit where one reviewer clocked Jarvis' 'hideous' yellow-orange jumper with the black trim, and Steve's broken ankle (with no mention of how he got it). Of the old songs, they only played 'Master Of The Universe' and 'They Suffocate at Night' amongst nine new songs, including an instrumental opener partly played on the stylophone, by the name of 'Space'. Space oddities indeed . . .

Another review noted: 'They sound positive now and demand attention.' Attention was also paid to the decorations – 'bubbles, yards of tin foil, glowing orange globes, a slide projector and cine film of motor racing' – and the vocalist's between-song patter. 'That song was about dying,' said Jarvis Cocker. 'Actually, this next one's about dying as well.' The review's conclusion? 'Pulp used to be interesting. Now they're wicked.'

As chance would have it, Pulp were asked to play *Sounds'* 1988 Christmas party, alongside The Membranes, through Robin Gibson, who was now on *Sounds'* staff. Dave Bedford was among the seasonal revellers. Even though Pulp were a bit before his time at Fire, he had always thought them a much better group than *Freaks* suggested and felt that 'Jarvis was always a star'. After the show, he struck up a conversation with the group which led to a 'come and see us again' resolution. 'I thought, "no chance",' said Jarvis. 'But nobody else was interested and so, to my eternal regret, we talked to Fire again.'

In Robin Gibson's mind, the fact that Pulp returned to Fire was proof they couldn't have been so badly treated in the first place. According to Dave Bedford, 'Fire had more money, new technology was cheaper, so it transpired that Pulp could make the record they wanted to make.'

Clive Solomon had been narked that Pulp had walked away the first time but was genuinely excited when they returned: 'I still loved them, and thought they were still being ignored.' This time, though, Pulp wanted a one-off single deal. Solomon pushed for, and got, a long term deal (for five albums), and the rights to reissue Pulp's back catalogue on CD.

True to form, things took time to work out. Fire had decided they didn't want to use the FON material so in July 1989, after college term was over, Pulp emerged from Priority Studios in Sheffield with a new six-track demo. The relationship with Dave Taylor obviously hadn't suffered too badly because the group shifted over to FON Studios in August to start work on a new album. According to Suzanne Catty, their future manager, 'Dave felt he had let them down badly, so he fronted them some studio time.'

The budget was £10,000, which Solomon thought large by Fire's standards – 'even today,' he reckons. 'Given the pressures of studies and work (Candida had already lost her first job because of band commitments, although another toy shop had been willing to employ her), Pulp were only able to record through the holidays and spare weekends, and only completed the sessions in December. At one point, Russell had even threatened to leave. 'Everything had just got too much,' Nick recalls, so it was fitting that Jarvis christened the nine-track set *Separations*. Final mixes were completed in January 1990. Welcome to the new decade!

8

my life with barry white

As if Pulp were celebrating the onset of the 90s, the group took their first dabble in the world of dance remixes just after *Separations* was finished. Sheffield DJs Parrot and Winston did two versions of 'This House Is Condemned', sampling Russell's robotic vocal and adding new beats (the second mix was renamed 'Is This House?'). Primitive and a bit stiff, neither were outstanding, and they were to sit in the can for over a year. Welcome to the new decade, evidently much the same as the old one . . .

In truth, Jarvis was a much happier, more balanced individual. London was an open field of possibilities, there was a new album completed, and the climate simply felt better. 'The 80s were generally a decade when a lot of people got excluded,' he reflected in 1992. 'It was basically an "I'm all right, just look after yourself and fuck everybody else" kind of message that was coming through, so anything of any real worth in the 80s came from the underground. Everybody had to dig themselves into the fall-out shelter and wait until the 80s were over, and we're only getting past that now.'

As he elaborated to *Vox*: 'The 80s should have been an important time, my twenties, an era of expansion. I wanted it to be exciting because I was born in the 60s and you look at the old films and it seems really good, all those parties. Now, suddenly, it's your time and everything's gone matt black and grey and people are saying: "Right, you've had yer fun, that's enough permissiveness, back to Victorian values."

'The 90s felt like life had begun again. I didn't blame any one single factor or person, or the occurrence of sunspots, or entering the age of Aquarius, y'know. It just became much nicer and simpler.'

We know how things turned out, but 1990 itself was Pulp's year of living dangerously – as they were in danger of disappearing altogether. There were no records, no concerts, nothing happening. Piecing together the evidence, it seems to be old news – FON had fronted studio time to Pulp, which Fire hadn't paid for because Pulp hadn't signed the final contracts. It wasn't until Christmas that they played a secret concert at Sheffield Leadmill, supporting those new Sheffield sensations World Of Twist. It was the first proper unveiling of the disco-matic Pulp, Russell's wah-wah pedal and all.

Once again, Jarvis had had ample time to dwell on his studies, and especially the short film he had to complete in his final year. He had been inspired by a church he'd seen in Mile End with a board that featured the slogan THIS IS THE GATE OF HEAVEN. 'I thought, that can't be what it looks like inside, a grotty church in the East End.' And, suitably impressed, he was off.

As he explained to *Select*, the film concerned an angel who comes down in human form to retrieve Gabriel's crown which has fallen off. 'On contact with earth, the crown had turned into a shower cap. She goes into a café and eats chips and curry sauce, then someone offers her a cigarette and she looks around, sees a bloke with one behind his ear and so that's what she does with it. Someone eventually puts the shower cap on and it dissolves in the bath because the cap is magic, so the cap gets thrown away. The angel, disheartened, falls asleep in a box and gets picked up and thrown out in a dustbin. When she wakes up, she finds the shower cap among the rubbish. It turns into a crown. She finds a church and tries to get in but it's locked. She turns around, looks at the camera and lights a cigarette. She says, "Oh, well" and walks off. And I would imagine that some of you might believe this reflects my views on life. You might be right.'

Jarvis was on his way to a 2:1. What a guy.

Eventually, in March 1991, with Parrot and Winston remixes propping up the rear, Pulp cemented their new direction with 'My Legendary Girlfriend'. From Scott Walker to Barry White wasn't a leap many groups made but Pulp always followed their own noses, and happily embraced extremes. The track opened with two and a half minutes of charged Philly-soul drama, *whacka-whacka* 'Shaft' guitar, reedy strings and Jarvis' deep-breathing, sweaty murmur, before it burst into an upbeat, rousing chorus. Jarvis' lovelorn images, in the bedroom and on the Sheffield street, were equally delivered with more detailed drama. '*So I woke her, and we went walking through the sleeping town, down deserted streets, frozen gardens grey in the moonlight, fences, down to the canal, creeping slowly past the cooling towers, deserted factories, looking for adventure / I wander the streets calling your name.*' Idealistic love had even turned to ideal lust: '*And the moon came on his face. It shone right through the clothes she wore. It shone right through the dress she wore. Good God!*'

Dynamic, cheesy, camp and totally driven, 'My Legendary Girlfriend' was sensational. It was always going to be touch and go which writer would review the singles on any given week, and *Melody Maker* were a little ungenerous: 'The first 30 seconds of this single are very very steamy indeed . . . and then the damn fool spoils it all by opening his mouth another centimetre or two, and singing. Worse – singing like Bryan Ferry was today's news, instead of World Of Twist.'

Ouch. World Of Twist had made a splash touting a loopy, 70s-tinged pop-disco mix and, as Jarvis ascerbically noted, silver-foil-decorated stage sets. Sounds familiar? Actually, World Of Twist were loads of fun, daft as brushes, with more of an electronic edge than Pulp – there was ample room in the world for both. But the comparison would have hurt; here was another group zooming past them, and the fact that Pulp had returned to Sheffield to support World Of Twist must have been hard to swallow.

Back from the wilderness; Pulp in 1991

(*Ed Sirrs*)

But hold the front page! 'My Legendary Girlfriend' became their first *NME* Single Of The Week. 'A throbbing ferment of night-club soul and teen opera,' it raved. 'Mysterious and grand.' An *NME* live review from Steve Lamacq, future 1FM DJ and then indie champion, was supportive too: 'Pulp meantime continue their resurrection as oddities, just on the right side of madness . . . Pulp are top entertainment, with lots lurking underneath.'

What's more, the single sold over 1500 copies, which thrilled the group no end – their popularity was growing for the first time, not shrinking.

Extra-curricular activity was being stepped up as well. The group had taken to handing out flyers at shows, to create the atmosphere of a club. 'Forty-four Pulpish Things To Do' included: 'wearing suede trousers with nothing on underneath';

Pulp, under starter's orders, from the same 1991 photo-session
(*Ed Sirrs*)

'doing a wheelie on a Raleigh Chopper'; 'not using words like quintessential, gig or basically'; 'going to the supermarket in a Lurex jumper'; 'being very knowledgeable about antique glass'; and so on. Fun was on the agenda; truth and beauty could look after themselves.

Jarvis and Russell were also more flippant during the new round of interviews. The notorious grumpiness was noticeably absent (probably left behind on a train between Sheffield and London), replaced by irreverent quips. In *NME*, they talked of supermarket prices and motorway service stations; in *Melody Maker*, Jarvis announced that 'getting in touch with Barry White is the thing because, as you know, he is quite spiritual. So if you tune into his wavelength, it's possible to get that sound, even without the Love Unlimited Orchestra.' His film course was a great diversion because 'music gets too much on my nerves when I do it too much. Overall, I prefer music because there's more chance of meeting nice girls. More opportunities to show off handling a microphone. I live in hope, anyway.'

Jarvis wasn't joking, though, when he told the *Sheffield Star* that he was still nurturing the ambition to make money. 'I know that sounds bad but when you end up with nothing or even less than when you started, you have got to have something a little more reliable . . . I've given rock'n'roll the best years of my life.'

While tuning into the Barry White wavelength, Jarvis still reserved an ear for Scott Walker. Despite the seemingly obvious solo Scott influences, Jarvis had only heard the Walker Brothers' huge, Spector-style ballads and Scott's bland MOR chart hits, but in 1987, he was lent the missing link, a tape of Scott's more intense, challenging solo work that Julian Cope, Marc Almond and other post-punk stars had raved about. Walker's work proved to be an important influence on Jarvis. 'I loved how he blended the poetic with the everyday, something I'd never heard done as well before. He was trying to say something about everyday life rather than just rhyming "moon" with "June" all the time. It was a real revelation. It inspired me to try harder with my own song-writing – but remember, reality is something you can't fake.'

The lyric to 'My Legendary Girlfriend' was definitely an example of everyday life taken to poetic extremes. Despite the cinematic bravura and detail, it was actually based on his girlfriend in Sheffield. 'See, I've never liked to mix business with pleasure. I've always kept my private life separate from music. So I've always gone out with girls who aren't interested in music, and so people are always asking me about my legendary girlfriend, because they've never seen me with her.'

Jarvis was keen to pinpoint 'mundane everyday things that assume the status of high art. I used to get too precious about our records and think they'd alter peoples' lives – I'd try too hard. Now I've mellowed. I'm simmering down . . . making records is just like bricklaying, and if people are impressionable, that's up to them.'

Irony No.1: as Jarvis moved to London, so Pulp's music shifted closer to the archetypal 80s Sheffield sound, fusing pop and dance with arch intent and arched eyebrows.

Irony No.2: despite being upstaged, World Of Twist made it easier for Pulp as reviewers finally had a reference point they had lacked before. London listings weekly *Time Out* also described Pulp as 'in the style of an updated, more eccentric Human League with indie cred', which made Pulp sound modern, and deep besides.

Irony No.3: as soon as Pulp stopped trying hard to make an impression, more people jumped on board. Or was it that, by sounding ironic as well as implying it, people were finally getting the point? Pulp no longer looked ironic either – the zeitgeist had come their way. In fashion terms, 70s 'naff' was coming into its own, a decade where the liberal advances of the 60s had both got out of hand, and gone back on itself, a decade whose odd, skew-whiff nature had proved its best quality. Feathercuts, platform boots, spacehoppers . . . we wouldn't really want to make them a

Balls to Pulp's detractors; Jarvis on stage at The Leadmill, Sheffield 1991

(*Mary Scanlon*)

Russell ignores Jarvis' shot-putting at the same Leadmill show
(Mary Scanlon)

part of our modern lives but it felt preferable to 80s values. (Greed, wedge haircuts, technological advances. You get my point.) Jarvis' tank-topped, wing-tipped, crimplened, slightly flared presence – a rock'n'roller out of a Scooby Doo cartoon – needed no falsification, or preparing. Once painfully unhip, now perversely hip, no way was Jarvis bandwagonesque.

The off-stage image was given plenty of on-stage opportunities to make an indelible impression. His stage presence had developed into a whirling dervish, illuminated by hand movements, part Alvin Stardust, part Ziggy Stardust. Shirley Bassey would have approved. These moves were straight out of the cabaret circuit, with sashaying hips to boot, while the spontaneous between-song patter had got drier and more deadpan to match the mood. Jarvis was making the kind of moves you might practise in front of the bedroom mirror, except that he was on stage, and made it look natural. Ironic and sincere, then. Cheesy and then some.

With his time taken up managing the moderately in-demand All About Eve as well as the more successful Mission, Tony Perrin had lost sight of Pulp, but he bumped into them at *Sounds'* Christmas party, and was smitten all over again. 'Jarvis was into his James Brown headtrip, which for some strange reason made perfect sense. He'd gone from a gangling, awkward, insecure kid out of school toward this kind of disco sex god. It was a revelation, and the crowd were going for it, including thirty or forty young girls down the front. I later saw them at the University of London, in front of 500 people, and they just blew the place apart. The key to their success was putting them in front of a crowd, and then building an audience.'

Melody Maker also witnessed the new Jarvis Love Machine first hand. '"New songs," muses frontman Jarvis Cocker, in answer to an impatient request from the front. "Yes, we've got lots of new songs, just to prove that our creative juices haven't dried up."'

'"We want juice," screamed one of the handful of women who

spent the best part of the night urging the singer to get his trousers off. "Hey," deadpans Jarvis, with a slight twist of his right hip. "We're gonna give you juice, baby." '

In the interim, Dave Bedford had managed to get Pulp a booking agent for the first time (the suitably named Wasted Talent), which enabled them to pick up progressively better shows, and bear out Tony Perrin's words. Says Bedford, 'Jarvis was such a star, so when they started developing a good following, it gave the press justifiable reason to cover them more comprehensively, plus people knew Jarvis out and about in London. Musically, too, people were finally catching up with them.'

Live reviews continued to increase the stakes. 'In normal life, singer Jarvis is probably just another skinny wretch with a personality crisis and hairdressing problem, but on stage, in his ludicrous stack heels and fluffy top, he assumes the holy status of a Big Elv. Captivating, excruciating and outrageously (un)sexy . . .' read one of the best. 'Ce groupe est un miracle,' wrote French monthly *Les Inrockuptibles*. 'Jarvis Cocker is an aspiring star. That's no startling revelation, just an inevitable fact,' said *NME*. 'To hell with careful qualification, Pulp are magic and Jarvis is a star,' said *Melody Maker*. 'Pulp are a flaming spaceship returning to a time when dancing wasn't just exercise with cigarettes . . . And Jarvis Cocker, in case you missed the clues, is God,' announced *Select*. Evidently calling Jarvis a star wasn't enough to describe his increasing All-Encompassingness . . .

9

10, 9, 8, 7, 6, 5, 4, 3, 2, 1, hold on a minute

Such tablets of wisdom had been brought down from the mountain before – remember the 'better than The Smiths' claim? – but never all at once. They were also singled out at the *NME*-sponsored 'Class Of 91' show at London's Town & Country club (which Central TV filmed) alongside Pale Saints, Midway Still and Kingmaker, and they kickstarted a sizeable fan base in France when they supported Blur and Lush a month later at the *Les Inrockuptibles* festival in Lille.

It looked like Pulp's moment had come, an 'AT LAST' sign enshrined in flashing disco lights, timed just right as Jarvis' three-year St Martin's course was coming to an end. Fire wanted another single to precede the new album, so the group went back into the studio and remixed 'Countdown'. Released at the end of May, it simply didn't have the same knockdown effect as 'My Legendary Girlfriend', despite a far snappier remix (compare it to the relatively lumpy 'Death Goes To The Disco' on the B-side) and a more conventionally structured, radio-friendly shaker than 'My Legendary Girlfriend'. There was no Single Of The Week, no new ground broken, just a step sideways rather than one forward.

Jarvis' lyrics couldn't have been more timely, the effect more ironic. '*I was seventeen when I heard the countdown start,*' Jarvis wailed, launching into what sounded like a desperate love song but was really a disguise for his feelings. Years ago, he felt his life was stalling on the launching pad yet years later, here he was still, and not much to show in the interim. '*Wasting all my time on all those stupid things that only get me down . . . I've gotta leave this town/ I'm not gonna hang around,'* he threatened.'I'd spent years on the dole, lying on my bed, thinking my time would come and it suddenly occurred to me that maybe it wouldn't,' he recalls. 'The years go by with you thinking, Well, when am I going to get to the 10,9,8,7,6 bit? It just never comes along and I began to think I'd wasted all this valuable time.'

With Fire lacking the promotional punch to make any kind of bigger splash, and most audience eyes locked on Grunge (Nirvana, almost anything American with hair) and Shoegazing (Lush, Ride, Chapterhouse, *et al.*), Pulp were still anomalies. You could hardly start a fire with profits from 1500 sales.

At least Jarvis was making use of his film course. The videos to 'My Legendary Girlfriend' and 'Countdown' were both completed with help from the college, knowing or otherwise. The former was done in one of St Martin's photo studios after the original East End pub footage was badly underlit, with Nick playing a cardboard drumkit as the budget didn't stretch to bringing the real one down from Sheffield.

'Countdown' was filmed on stage at the Leadmill but fiddled with to compensate for the footage's bad exposure, and then edited at the same time as Jarvis' graduation film, which Steve was producing. Says Jarvis, 'This involved the extreme step of hiding in a stock cupboard in the college so that we could edit overnight after the caretaker had locked up. It was during one of these sessions that my fellow editor, Martin Wallace, was forced to "go to the toilet" in a carrier bag as a trip to the toilets would have involved setting off the burglar alarm.'

Yet these collective calamities were the least of Pulp's problems. More time had been spent revamping 'Countdown', which made it almost eighteen months since *Separations* had been finished. The fickle finger of fate struck once again – as Fire finally set a release date, the label's record distributors, Rough Trade, declared bankruptcy, forestalling all releases.

Jarvis, Steve and Nick on a Thames away-day for *Sounds* magazine, 1991
(*Mary Scanlon*)

In Dave Bedford's mind, both Pulp and Fire were to blame. He cited as an example the fact that Pulp were slow at sending in the album artwork, but when they did, Clive Solomon returned the computer disc to Sheffield because it would cost more to process than finished artwork. Yet Bedford acknowledges that, had Fire got on with things, the album could have been released six months before Rough Trade collapsed. 'When Rough Trade went under, I know the band were fairly gutted. We all were. For six months, we couldn't do anything, as we lost close to £100,000 and it was almost all over.'

Faced with even more time to consider their position, Pulp decided that a third of the LP wasn't up to scratch. In their minds, it had dated, plus they had better songs. 'Everyone felt the second half of the album was weak in places,' remembers Bedford.

At which juncture, enter Suzanne Catty. Russell and Tony Perrin had discussed the possibility of working together again. 'Though it never came to fruition, it was funny because he blamed me for fucking Pulp up in the first place for making *It*!' says Perrin. But Catty, then Simon Hinkler's girlfriend, had seen Pulp in Sheffield and immediately wanted to manage them.

'They had unbelievable talent and as much potential,' she enthuses. 'It was insane that they weren't selling records. Jarvis was clearly one of the most talented, classic stars of the last twenty, thirty years. I could see him fill stadiums even then. I could see him as Frank Sinatra. I believed I could make the band one of the biggest things on the planet.'

The Canadian-born Catty had valuable major label experience in the international department at Phonogram, working with groups like Def Leppard, Metallica and Was (Not Was), and at Hollywood Records. Russell, Pulp's business brains, encouraged the relationship, and so Catty, full of self-belief as well as Pulp-belief, left Hollywood and set up her own company, Curve Ball Management, in Sheffield.

With industry contacts intact, Catty had a direct line to A&R departments, and despite sceptical reactions to a band over a decade old, she was able to whip up interest in Pulp. She hassled the booking agent for better shows; Pulp did a dozen in and around London in four months and got more money for each as the crowds grew. 'It's not enough that people love the band,' Catty maintained. 'You need a team effort working towards a common goal to get anywhere in the business.'

Catty also admits to putting pressure on the group too. 'It wasn't that they were lazy but after ten years of wanting it so bad but never believing it would happen, you're frightened to commit in case you get heartbroken again. Needless to say, they rose to the occasion.'

Catty rose to the occasion as well, by acting the muscly manager and claiming that Pulp were free of their contract from Fire, and available to be signed. Fire were unaware of her plot, and had already agreed to Pulp's demands for money to update *Separations*, as the label had a new distribution deal in place and an advance of money. The label sat back and waited . . . and waited, but, as Dave Bedford says, six months passed without Pulp delivering. 'We'd speak to Suzanne about the sessions and she'd say the studio had broken down, or Steve had a cold. In the end, I rang FON and found they hadn't made a booking in ages, so she was lying. And then we heard she'd started talking to other labels.'

Fire were naturally enraged. 'There aren't many people in the world I hate,' Dave Bedford reflects, 'but if I saw her walking in the road, I'd run her over. She thought she knew it all, and she took a very adversarial stance even before she met us. All she wanted was to sign Pulp to a major deal and make money. She and Jarvis knew all along that things took time and Fire's aim was to license Pulp internationally, but the band were probably desperate and she was promising them the earth. And while I felt Fire was badly treated, the label's limitations proved too much in

**Jarvis dares you to laugh at his jacket. Nick wonders what possessed
Jarvis to wear it. Steve just wants to borrow it**
(Mary Scanlon)

the end. Clive was never in the business of risking money, which
I guess is why all the best bands left.'

Catty says she didn't try and pull the wool over anyone's eyes.
She believed Pulp had definite grounds for divorce, and for
notifying Fire that the label was in breach of the second contract,
and of the contract that Pulp originally signed with them. 'I don't
know if Fire had ever sent the band a royalty statement in their
lives!' she claims. 'I thought Fire's contracts were horrendous too
– it seemed impossible for bands to make a penny, and since Fire
had delayed *Separations* for so long, the lawyers said that we had a
very positive case if we could fight it. The band knew every detail
and were happy to continue.'

The opportunity arose to call Fire's bluff by releasing a single
through a new Sheffield label, Gift. Rob Mitchell and Steve
Beckett had formed Warp, a techno label running out of the

renowned shop of the same name, who had already got Jarvis and Steve to make promo videos for two Warp releases (Nightmares On Wax's 'Aftermath' and Sweet Exorcist's 'Testone'). The Warp boys wanted to start an indie label, and after Catty had approached them, they realized Pulp were a perfect beginning. For the group, it meant a chance to start again while Catty negotiated a major label deal.

At the end of 1991, 'My Legendary Girlfriend' was voted number 31 in *NME*'s Top 50 Singles poll. That Kylie Minogue's 'What Do I Have To Do' came 32nd might, or might not, shed some light on how significant this really was, but it seemed a good omen nevertheless. On 28 January 1992, Pulp trouped back into FON Studios and recorded four new tracks with Simon Hinkler back in the producer's chair. Passing over new stage favourites like 'My First Wife', 'Heart Trouble' and 'Going Back To Find Her', they plumped for 'O.U. (Gone, Gone)', 'Space', 'Live On' and 'Babies'.

No wonder Pulp had wanted to revamp *Separations* if this was the direction they were taking – the demo could have been a different group altogether, with distinctly glammy and poppy edges, spacier keyboards and a fuller, more integrated sound. A totally new group, in fact, in a different class altogether. Typically for wilful buggers like Pulp, dance had gone in the direction of techno and technology grown more sophisticated but Pulp were heading back to a more 70s definition of disco and the quirky, analogue sounds of the 70s Moog synthesizer. Countdown had begun! Well, nearly.

10

rock'n'roll, i've given you the best years of my life

As a member of Island Records' A&R team, Nigel Coxson's brief was to keep eyes peeled for every opportunity. No one could have failed to see Pulp's emergence from obscurity, or the fact that Jarvis was starting to appear in the more gossipy pages of the music press. He could see that the Manchester/ 'Madchester' scene (The Stone Roses, Happy Mondays, indie-dance anthems, flares, loads of E, crazed personalities) had died away, and that the Shoegazing scene (Ride, Slowdive, Chapterhouse, drug-rock anthems, drainpipes, lots of staring down at shoes, zero personalities) lacked real dynamism. Suede were just emerging, trailing more poppy, grandiose songs and an old-fashioned concept of pop glamour, playing with the camera instead of gazing down at their feet, and Pulp had a similarly timely feel. They even had a one-word name.

Jarvis: 'Dave Gilmour was the first Island A&R man to see us, and he got Nigel to see us play outside Wolverhampton. We were supporting The Primitives, of all groups, and we were really shit. It was one of those nights advertising, "Budweiser £1 a pint plus band", so everyone was in the bar getting hammered, including us. We thought we'd blown it but he liked it.'

Nigel Coxson: 'I'd heard songs like "My Legendary Girl-friend", "Countdown", even "Little Girl (With Blue Eyes)", and thought they were good but not great. But the new ones I heard, like "Babies", were classic, unusual songs, and very different to what else was going on. I wasn't put off by how long they had been going as a lot of bands take time before they come to fruition, although I suppose it was a brave decision to follow them up in the sense that nobody else particularly seemed to think they were that good – they seemed more of a critics' band. People thought it was all a bit tongue in cheek, that the band needed some development, but I thought Jarvis was already a complete star.'

'Countdown' may have been a flop but Pulp on stage, with their spanking-new songs, was still an event, and their own coterie of fans was slowly on the up. The group knew that the stage was, up to this point, their best chance, and they worked on it accordingly.

Russell: 'We do have these ridiculous little vibing up sessions, where we exclude everyone from the dressing room and get into a bit of a huddle. I don't want to go into that too much 'cos I don't think you should see behind the scenes, to see the swan's feet clicking away underneath the swan gliding on the surface, but we've always tried to break on through to the other side, one way or another, and elevate it beyond a band just having good songs. We used to do it more in the past, as we were very intense on stage, better than on record until *Different Class*. But this is not some clever invention. We sat and wrote all this world plan down, when things started going for us again. We were seriously trying to be the number one band in the world.'

In Russell's mind, the fact that Pulp were approaching lift-off was much more to do with Jarvis' behaviour on stage than the music. 'One thing that would infuriate me about him was that he's always been a brilliant performer but he used to undermine it by taking the piss out of himself. He'd work up the audience and then be self-effacing and say, "We are crap." If there was a little sound problem, he'd go over to the sound engineer and threaten to smack him, and other ridiculous little absurd theatrics that didn't look dark and intense but kind of stupid. Things had built up but then fizzled out a bit, and we were still playing

The first photo session for Gift, 1992

(Colin Bell)

depressingly sad gigs to seventy people in London, and we were just shooting ourselves in the foot with that attitude.

'I almost had this argument with Jarvis, being pissed off with him for not being a proper pop star, and it seemed like the group would split up at that time. And then, for some reason, it started feeling pretty good, pretty much overnight. He stopped doing the "I am a crap, speccy git", and seriously tried to be a proper pop star, and sexy, rather than a parody of a pop star. I think he knew that we couldn't just carry on in our own little underground way, held together with a rubber band, so he started taking it seriously.'

Warner's subsidiary East West Records were also keen to sign Pulp but the group got on better with Nigel Coxson, and the decision was made. Island were ready to make an offer by the time Pulp and Gift had agreed the group was to release a single. Says Rob Mitchell, 'We didn't have the money to keep Pulp but we decided to take a gamble and release a single as a stepping stone to get Gift going, and to give Pulp a chance to raise their heads above the parapet and see if Fire would fire.'

Pulp originally intended to make 'Live On' the A-side though 'O.U. (Gone Gone)' won out – the former was possibly too close a rewrite of Gloria Gaynor's disco anthem 'I Will Survive' for comfort, though their future press officer John Best reckoned the group thought it sounded too much like Bruce Springsteen for their liking! 'O.U.', meanwhile, was a glistening, perky nugget.

All they had to do was overcome what the group thought was a weak production from Simon Hinkler. They turned to producer Ed Buller; Steve and Jarvis had been impressed with his work on Suede's just released debut single 'The Drowners' and his ability to layer keyboards and guitar on Spiritualized's ambitious *Lazer Guided Melodies* album. 'Ed did one remix and it sounded like a real record for the first time,' Steve reckoned, and with a June release, Pulp were off to yet another big new beginning. The title 'O.U.' was perfect – the initials stood for 'Open University', because the group thought the opening synth melody reminded them of a theme for an Open University programme.

The song's guitar chords were familiar too, as they reprised those from the 1986 EP track '97 Lovers' yet 'O.U. (Gone Gone)' was chalk to the former's cheese. Though Jarvis' lyric was still locked into relationship/communication breakdown, his tone was more casual, almost insouciant – *'The night was ending, he needed her undressed, he said he loved her, he tried to look impressed'* – and not centred around himself, unless Jarvis was the man who, on hearing his girlfriend walking out for good at eight o'clock in the morning, was faced with the decision to leap up and stop her or catch another hour's kip. He probably was, you know.

The B-side was 'Space', starring the stylophone (the tinny keyboard-with-metal-pen that Rolf Harris popularized and David Bowie used on *Space Oddity*). Here, Jarvis summed up the onset of the new and the passing of the old – *'Did you ever think this day would happen? After days of trying to sell washing machines in the rain?/It looked like we'd never leave the ground but we're weightless, floating free, we can go wherever we want'* – but then recognizing that you can't survive in space or in dreamland – *'Space is OK but I'd rather get my kicks down below.'* At which point, the music shifts from the drifting, whooshing Moogs into a stabbing, thrilling rockout. *Yowsa!*

Even more than 'My Legendary Girlfriend', 'O.U. (Gone Gone)' looked like Pulp's reprieve. The press were overwhelmingly on their side this time – a Single Of The Week in *Melody Maker* ('this is colossal . . . three minutes of staggering poptasm') and a rave in *NME* was backed up by live reviews, now Pulp were playing more shows than ever, as well as their mini-festival appearances.

Money was so tight that there was no cash for a video, although the group had managed to enlist an independent PR company. Savage & Best had started making good with Suede, and were willing to take Pulp on in the expectation of being paid when the group was famous, of which they had little doubt.

Pulp had been introduced to John Best through the group's friendship with Lush – vocalist Miki Berenyi was John's then girlfriend. There was already a connection of sorts: John's partner Phill Savidge (notice different spelling – 'if we spelt it Savidge & Best, we'd look like a firm of solicitors', he emphasizes) shared a flat in Nottingham with Peter Dalton.

'Like everyone else in the industry, when I was working as a journalist, I'd made a snap assessment of Pulp in 1986, thinking they were all right,' John Best recalls. 'Miki had played with them and Blur in France, and came back saying Pulp were brilliant, and had come on a long way. When we met, I found them more accommodating as people than most other bands, with humility and a hunger. After being unsuccessful for that long, you can't hold that many airs and graces. They were happy for the attention.'

John Best, Phill Savidge and Melissa Thompson, who ended up handling the day-to-day running of Pulp's press, were based in Camden Town, which was becoming the hub of a rapidly evolving London-based scene that was fast replacing the Thames Valley Shoegazers and 'Madchester'. The company were connected in a way that Amrik Rai never was, as the groups they handled (Suede, Elastica and The Verve among them) were good friends with myriad other groups in London, and they had wider contacts with the music press. The good thing was, Pulp were in no danger of losing their identity; the group was still the maverick of the pack, individual to the core.

Not that Pulp were immediately considered Next Big Thing material. John Best: 'Pulp are the most gratifying project we've ever worked on because journalists never gave a shit at first. It was all so parochial and small-time when we started – everything was on a very amateur-dramatic level, like these gilt picture frames they'd made with second-hand shoes glued to them and sprayed gold. They must have been really bored! But they at least put the effort in and cared a lot. They knew how to depend on themselves with no money around.'

When it came to the art of building an image, the company made a point of separating Jarvis in both photo shoots and interviews. John Best: 'We felt that early interviews and pictures involving all of them had only cluttered their image, with garbled chatter about crimplene and spangles and chopper bikes and out-of-sync 70s nostalgia coming through. People thought Jarvis was a comedian and taking the piss but knowing him personally, we knew there was a lot more going on than such surface fripperies. Lyrically, he had great conviction so it was very frustrating to talk to the *NME* and hear them described as 70s revivalists like Denim, like they were kitsch. Jarvis had a kernel of something far more heartfelt.'

The group were equally frustrated by the accusations of kitsch – that they were celebrating the inferior or bad-taste elements of their chosen art. Pulp undoubtedly understood and appreciated kitsch but it was far from their overriding aesthetic.

'People think if you don't take everything seriously, then you're not as meaningful,' Steve told *The List*. 'Because we do things like try and make our sleeves and our videos interesting, and wear certain types of clothes, people think it means there's less content. If anything, it's the opposite, because it means you're thinking about what you're doing.'

The group's nerves showed through in the odd interview. In *What's On* magazine, Russell said, 'Sometimes I feel like we're on death row and we keep getting reprieves. I just want to shout, "Oh God, just fucking kill us or reprieve us. One or the other! Anything to end this horrible, horrible nightmare!"'

In interviews, the group would treat 1991 as Year Zero. Russell talked of 'our hideous past' and hoped fans hadn't heard their old records, as if the horrors of the past outweighed their still considerable achievements.

Pulp knew they had to keep working hard on the live set, and

Jarvis singled out in Sheffield, 1992

(*Kevin Westenberg*)

so they started using their tour manager Mark Webber as a second guitarist. Known as Zig to all and sundry (and credited so on Pulp sleeves), Mark used to follow fellow Fire signings Spacemen 3 around before running a psychedelic club in Sheffield known as The Groovy Fish Tank. He first saw Pulp at his local arts centre in Chesterfield, when Jarvis was in his wheelchair, and interviewed the group for his fanzine. He subsequently made friends with them over the years, progressing from assisting their light shows to running their fan club *Disco-Very* and to the lofty position of tour manager. Playing live with them was the stuff that dreams are made of.

Pulp were finally making a habit of working with the right people but the relationship with Suzanne Catty had started deteriorating. For some reason – a lack of judgement? Desperation? A capacity for self-destruction? – Pulp had a tendency to work with people they would eventually regret even talking to. Catty was definitely one of them, but like the others, she was driven by a fierce belief in Pulp, and they were motivated by her commitment. 'She was the first person ever to say, "I can make you stars, and by Christmas," 'Russell remembers. 'She's probably my most mortal enemy on Earth now but you have to give her the credit for saying it.'

Suzanne Catty had started making enemies of the group when the delicate nature of business intruded. Arguments escalated over choice of lawyers and the correct level of legal bills and, fearing that matters could go horribly awry, the group felt they had to find a way out of the mess.

On the advice of John Best, they went to see Geoff Travis, the man who had started Rough Trade Records, one of the first, and most influential, British independent labels, whose greatest achievement was signing The Smiths. (Though he remained on the board, Travis had given away the Rough Trade distribution company to the employees, and wasn't actively involved in the debacle that ended the latter.)

By accident more than design, Travis had branched out into management when The Cranberries came to see him for advice, and wasn't looking around for any other group to manage. 'I didn't really know anything about Pulp at the time but I went to see them play and absolutely loved them,' he recalls. 'In a funny way, they reminded me of a cross between The Rolling Stones and Manfred Mann, another classic UK pop band. They seemed to play one fantastic song after another, and as a front man, Jarvis is as good as they can be. I don't know why they were idling around for so long, and so I agreed to represent them.'

Jarvis: 'It was almost like Geoff took pity on us as we didn't have anything to offer him. We owed lots of money everywhere so we weren't an attractive proposition at all, but luckily Geoff is more interested in music than money. I remember coming out of his office after our first meeting, having talked for three hours, with a very big feeling of relief. He single-handedly restored my faith in the music business as I'd thought everyone before was quite horrible or a demon.'

Island were keen to sign Pulp but there was one snag – the group were still officially signed to Fire. A plan was hatched whereby Pulp would remain on Gift, but Island would finance the releases. The Island deal was signed, with the advance cheque being put in a safe until the problems with Fire were sorted out. On the day, Candida remembered her and Russell going out 'and buying some clothes with the £100 allowance we all got, and then spending loads of money in Safeway on this extravagant food, like peanut biscuits and Lapsang Souchong tea. I felt so sick but it was worth it.' Jarvis, meanwhile, couldn't find any clothes he liked so he went back to Oxfam.

That was on the Friday. The following Monday, with Travis on their side, Pulp sacked Catty. 'Jarvis said he had a cold so I had to do it,' Steve recalls. 'She had to be paid off but she tried to sue us for £40,000. We'd only signed a letter of intention for her to manage us as it wasn't legally binding. We said we'd give her

£4000 or to take us to court as we had no obligations, which she eventually accepted.'

Catty had the option to sue Pulp; in the end, she decided not to. 'I loved Pulp so why would I do anything to harm them?' Yet she feels maligned and mistreated. 'I'd got them the most killer publishing deal, better than million-selling bands would get, which will make them a lot of money even if they're paying Fire a royalty override, and I got them their major label deal. Why was I sacked? Certainly Russell and Steve had problems with me being female and North American, and they didn't like to hear things from me, and I wouldn't tolerate the usual nonsense.'

Rob Mitchell: 'Pulp had done what they'd done, in a low key way, for so long, it took someone else to point out that there was another way of doing it, like, "You're better than this, you need to believe in yourself." She was desperate to kick them up the arse, and took them right up to signing both the record and publishing deals. She was brilliant. But they sacked her because she had no idea of the style of the band. Her reference points were American AOR rock bands, which grated on them. She'd put forward the example of Right Said Fred as a band that were quirky but successful, whereas Jarvis' vision was Jacques Brel and Donna Summer, much more of a grandiose and soulful vision. It was cruel what they did but they couldn't have maintained a long relationship with someone they didn't see eye to eye with.'

The same scenario had, of course, developed with Fire. Unlike Suzanne Catty, Clive Solomon was willing to fight, to the group's detriment. He had let Gift release 'O.U.' but as soon as Island came on the scene, he started gearing up. With a legal background, Solomon wasn't about to be overwhelmed by any lawyers, even when Island got behind the case. 'You've entered into an agreement with someone and if you want out, you sit down and work it out rather than unilaterally tear the agreement up,' he objected. 'So I did all I could to resist it, for as long as it took.'

In Dave Bedford's mind, 'Clive had a big ego and felt insulted. He wanted to screw them for all he could get, even if it meant the band splitting up.'

But Solomon claims he was only working along the lines of law and principle. 'Disputes are horrible as I don't think I'd ever want to work with someone who didn't want to work with me, but it was a question of doing things a proper way.'

Steve: 'Suzanne Catty really kept us in the dark. We're now very literate in all aspects of the music business but back then, we just wanted to release a record, and she managed to bullshit us quite well into believing we could free ourselves without much hassle. She had that kind of Canadian/American, "they won't fuck with me" attitude, and she was so wrong.'

Suzanne Catty is still adamant that if it wasn't for the cowardice of Pulp's lawyers and the group, they would have won, but they were afraid of entering into deeper waters. 'The lawyers simply weren't aggressive enough whereas Fire had one of the toughest lawyers in the music business. Russell especially wouldn't risk things not panning out for the band, not with his house and baby. Over ten years, they had never had proper management and had become totally entrenched in their methodology – they dig their heels in but when the crunch comes, they cave in. Remember, people told them they walked on water and they were that talented, but they still got nowhere for all those years – why?'

It took a further two years of litigation before an agreement was reached, with Fire eventually settling for a system of royalty 'points' on Pulp's next four albums.

In the end, Solomon didn't take out an injunction against the group to stop them recording for Gift or signing to Island. 'I felt I'd been treated badly but didn't want to go as far as to prevent them from doing anything. When it came to putting out *Separations*, I remember being helpful about the date, waiting until after they'd released a new single.'

Whatever mistakes Pulp had made in the past, the band were determined to move onward and upward. Finally feeling settled with Island and with Geoff Travis handling the business side of life, they could move on and fulfil their vision – slightly flared, made of acrylic, and maddeningly catchy.

11

up, up and away

In Pulp-tastic style, the band had celebrated the release of 'O.U. (Gone Gone)' with the launch of hundreds of balloons on the recreation ground opposite Mr Kite's Wine Bar, with a local photographer in attendance. The balloons had address tags attached; the returnee who lived furthest away won a night with Jarvis in Camberwell. (The winner turned out to live in Slovenia so, sadly, the proposed evening never took place.)

Pulp made a slightly bigger splash when they set off on the group's very first official UK tour – in other words, a string of more than five shows. The tour was notable for including Pulp's first shows in Scotland, the sight of Jarvis playing the stylophone behind his head, *à la* Jimi Hendrix, and increasingly good reviews all round. The group stopped halfway through the tour to record a session for Radio 1's *Mark Goodier Show*, choosing 'Babies', 'Live On', 'Glass' and 'She's A Lady' for the occasion.

Though the 70s values of glamour and entertainment were definitely on the cultural agenda, it was clear that 70s kitschedelia alone – from tight crimplene to flapping collars, from *Star Trek* annuals to ancient Moog synths – wasn't going to make stars of anyone. World Of Twist had already faded, and Suede would never have created such fervour if the group had been simply Bowie clones. Pulp were even less of a retro concept, as any pop fan from the 70s could confirm that no group remotely resembled Pulp in sound or vision. Blur were to join in this concerted retaliation against Grunge and Shoegazing's anti-entertainment stance, and you could safely bet that Brett Anderson and Damon

Albarn had even cribbed a few stage tricks off Jarvis. But it was to fall to Suede to become the first British group who were good enough and ready enough to kickstart the pop-glamour 90s, armed with a sensational run of singles ('The Drowners', 'Metal Mickey', 'Animal Nitrate' and 'So Young') and Brett Anderson's bewitching persona.

John Best: 'Before Suede, flamboyancy was seen as a sell-out trait. A band like Spiritualized epitomized the attitude: if you were serious about your music, you didn't act showbusinessy as all that bollocks cheapens the art. But Suede picked up on the need for people to be entertained again. People always have an appetite for the next thing, and after the Shoegazing in the UK, which was good musically but dire in retrospect, people didn't want to be an American Grunge band. It's the *Zeitgeist*.'

And then, just as everything was *Zeitgeist*-fresh and forward-looking, Fire went ahead and released *Separations* in June.

Pulp had declined Fire's offer to buy the album back, it being so old, but for Fire, the timing was good. The music press treated the release with suspicion but couldn't deny the record's great strengths – and it had many, despite its flaws and its obvious raids from history's larder.

The title seemed to reflect the band's recent past, with Jarvis' failures on the girlfriend front and the fact that the group had been living in different cities. There had been the added frisson of Russell nearly departing, plus the gap between the album's recording and its release date. Now Pulp were totally separate from their own record. At least there was no shortage of irony.

Separations shared in *Freaks'* majestic broodiness but, musically and lyrically, displayed more variety and drama, with Pulp's gangly angle on dance music making for a cornucopia of quark, strangeness and charm. The opening 'Love Is Blind' was a perfect example – upbeat, spacious, with a thumping rock backbeat, but the same passionately wallowing Pulp and wailing Jarvis: '*So we kissed, and we laid on the bed, and we waited for the ceiling to fall in, but it never did/in the morning, it was still all there – the spilt milk and the dog turds.'*

'Don't You Want Me Anymore?' was a bit light-fingered. Its title resembled The Human League's 'Don't You Want Me', the intro was clearly that of Jacques Brel's 'Next' and the lyric *'I've never seen you look so ugly as the way you did that night'* a reverse of the sentiments in Chris de Burgh's hideous MOR smoothie 'Lady In Red'. But the track could only be Pulp.

'She's Dead' was an old-fashioned Pulp slowie, with a direct melodic and mood lift from 60s balladeer Bobby Goldsboro's weepie 'Honey', but where the former lamented an early death, Jarvis was only documenting the end of an affair.

The title track was Pulp by way of Cecil B. de Mille. Russell's grand Slavic violin intro lasted over a minute before Jarvis took over with a pure pulp-fiction portrayal of unrequited love (empty beds, lonely bar-room tables, the moon high in the sky, *'and the night is dark between them now'*). A see-sawing central motif, a neo-spaghetti-western atmosphere and another violin-soaked drama took the track to its finish. Gulp. 'Down By The River' was nearly 'Separations' part two, plumbing the Brel/Slavic depths and ending up with a fatalistic country blues that could have been Nick Cave or The Violent Femmes. End of side one. Take a breath.

Side two mined the momentary deformed/dislocated disco Pulp. 'Countdown' and 'My Legendary Girlfriend' were followed by 'Death II', a revamped version of 'Death Comes To Town', sounding like Boney M covering Gene Pitney's 'Something's Gotten Hold Of My Heart': *'Oh! Hey! Oh now the lonely nights begin and there is nowhere else left to go/but watch my spirit melt away down at the D-I-S-C-O/I must have died a thousand times.'* By the end, Jarvis is a neurotic mess.

The album ended with 'This House Is Condemned'. This was Russell's last stab at singing – 'Which I never liked, on account of having a really crap voice,' he reasons. Typically for Russell, the mood was claustrophobic and dank – the vocals and lyrics are spooked, the Acid House FX cheap, minimal but effective, with a piano break and electro-squiggles. Uneasy listening.

This was the closest Pulp came to an Acid House thumper. 'We tried to make Acid House,' confessed Steve, 'but apart from "My Legendary Girlfriend", they turned out awful because we were trying to find out about MIDI and didn't know what we were doing. We couldn't handle the technology, which was pretty sad.'

By the time *Separations* was released, technology was well under control, overseen by producers like Ed Buller. Yet the next Pulp artefact was from the under-stairs cupboard – a rehearsal of 'My Legendary Girlfriend' from the BBC's *Hit The North* session, 'Back in LA' from 1984's 'Ping Pong Jerry' demos and 1982's 'Sickly Grin' from their third ever set of demos – released as part of a 7" series on the Caff label, run by Bob Stanley, journalist and founder member of synth-pop artisans St Etienne.

Back on the real release schedule, in May, Pulp recorded a six-track demo in Island's Fallout Shelter, under Island's West London HQ, and then returned in July for five days and another in August working on the new single.

When they released 'Babies' in October, Pulp even felt positive enough to put a clear image of themselves on the cover for the first time – they'd always hidden behind graphic images or distorted group portraits before. But this was Pulp *au naturel* – Russell struck an especially voguish pose.

Originally titled 'Nicky's Song' (Nick had come up with the opening guitar chords), 'Babies' teemed with pure-pop confidence, mating another rousing chorus with the brilliantly funny, farcical scenario of Jarvis hiding in his schoolfriend's sister's wardrobe, listening to her having sex – *'I want to give you children, you might be my girlfriend, yeah'* – and then being caught in the act and ending up having sex with her. *'Oh listen, we were on the bed when you came home, I heard you outside the door, I know you won't believe it's true: I only went with her 'cos she looks like you.'*

In other words, not the kind of lyric you write when you crave radio play and commercial acceptance.

Of the B-sides, 'Styloroc (Nites Of Suburbia)' came from the May demo, but won its subtitle because Jarvis used lyrics from from 'Nites Of Suburbia', where Jarvis talked of such joys as *'spouting black hair beneath Bri-Nylon underwear'* and *'a thousand fake orgasms every night behind the thick Dralon curtains'*.

'Sheffield Sex City' was an eight-and-a-half-minute soap-operatic embellishment of the 'Styloroc' world, blending Sheffield, sex, suburbia, squalor and seediness ('the morning after "My Legendary Girlfriend"' Jarvis wrote on the sleeve). Over an electro-disco pulse in the vein of Donna Summer's throbathon 'Love To Love You Baby', Candida began by relaying a tale of, at the age of eleven, hearing a couple having sex on the other side of the bedroom wall.

Over the top, Jarvis began listing numerous nondescript Sheffield suburbs and surrounding districts ('Intake, Manor Park, The Wicker, Norton, Frecheville . . .') before unfolding a scene set between midnight and dawn – the procreating hour. If the old Pulp was *Freaks*, and 'Babies' was an echo of *Gregory's Girl*, then 'Sheffield Sex City' was (to borrow a description from Miranda Sawyer in the *Observer*) *'Saturday Night and Sunday Morning* and *Saturday Night Fever'*, with both the harsh realism of playright Mike Leigh, the cosier snapshots of comedienne Victoria Wood and the soap-operatic cadences of *Coronation Street*'s founder Tony Warren. *'Old women clacked their tongues in the shade of crumbling concrete bus shelters. Dogs doing it in central reservations and causing multiple pile-ups in the centre of town . . . everyone on Park Street came in unison at 4.13 a.m. and the whole block fell down. The tobacconist's caught fire and everyone on the street died of lung cancer. We heard groans coming from a T-reg Chevette. You bet . . .'*

Interesting fact: like Jarvis, Tony Warren grew up in a poor, matriarchal society, which made for sympathetic treatment of women and an acknowledgement of your roots. 'Adversity breeds background and telling comment,' Warren emphasized. Compared to 'Dogs Are Everywhere', Jarvis was now almost eulogizing the doggish characters. If you can't beat 'em, then join 'em . . .

Like 'My Legendary Girlfriend', where Pulp had tried invoking the spirit of Barry White, 'Sheffield Sex City' was the result of what Russell called, 'One of our little, weird barnstorming sessions where we'd turn the lights out and say, "Now let's create a certain mood." Like, let's imagine we're in a small seaside town and it's a pursuit, someone's hiding, or let's write a sexy song like "Sheffield Sex City", and get a certain atmosphere, but not be so weird that it wasn't pop music. In the early days, we just ended up being weird and dark but I genuinely think there's been less change in Pulp than a change in what people want out of a band.'

The result was a superbly slinky white-funk backdrop for Jarvis's particularly inspired heavy-breathing delivery. *All right.*

Melody Maker described 'Sheffield Sex City' as 'grotesque, sensuous, hopelessly misguided and thoroughly extraordinary' in the process of making 'Babies' Single Of The Week. Teen bible *Smash Hits* made it their Record *Du Jour* – 'A fantastic, imaginative and wonderful record . . . Pulp could well become the band of all our tomorrows.' These were comments which encouraged the belief that Pulp could have appeal beyond the indie-pop bubble.

'Babies' and 'Sheffield Sex City' saw Jarvis' lyrical powers achieve lift-off. By concentrating on the mundane everyday, the poetry had come into its own, and nailed down an original version of truth and beauty. A local journalist thought Cocker had caught Sheffield 'in all its run-down, overgrown-villagey, dirty, sleazy, warm-hearted, warts'n'all glory'.

'What got me about London was all the highs and lows,' Jarvis told *Melody Maker*. 'One minute you're sitting in this shitty little flat and the next you're in this flash club. But what struck me was how different people were, and how different the life was. To a lot of Londoners, the stuff me and my friends got up to in Sheffield seemed almost exotic. And I realized that all this stuff that had happened to me that I'd thought was dead normal was actually worth writing about.'

Jarvis reckoned he had started writing more about Sheffield when he'd moved away because he had no social life in London to distract him, and more to the point, he now had the necessary objectivity to realize how the city had shaped his life. But if Sheffield was clearly on his mind, he just as clearly had sex on the brain.

He had been site-specific and hormonally hung-up before – remember auntie and uncle doing it under Roger Moore's photo in '97 Lovers'? – but this three-track extravaganza was the beginning of Jarvis' new vocation as chronicler of the lust-struck and the sex-starved. He and Russell had once complained about groups thrusting their crotches in people's faces to become the Mike Yarwoods of pop (make that the Rory Bremners of pop now) and new technocrats selling sex to teenagers by way of fake romance, whereas Pulp was prepared to do it the proper way.

'By 1991, what struck me was how sexless pop music had become,' he told *Vox*. 'I thought I could see a gap in the market. I mean, sex is constantly on people's minds, isn't it, but in pop it's written about in such a nebulous way. Look at that Bank of England bloke . . . he's off to the job centre because of it.'

What really elevated Jarvis' depictions of Sheffield, sex and city life was Jarvis' attention to detail. Scott Walker's portrayal of a particularly unswinging 60s London included incidental details and place names but Jarvis was even more taken by author/journalist Tom Wolfe, writer of the American epics *Bonfire Of The Vanities* and *The Right Stuff*.

'Details are things that reveal something bigger,' Jarvis told the *Observer*. 'They give authenticity. I realized that when I read Tom Wolfe's journalism as he went into obsessive detail but it revealed a person's character. You can tell a lot about somebody if they're wearing really bad shoes, or something frayed, or they keep scratching the inside of their hand. And I always wanted to write songs about love and sex, but not those ones that give you a false impression that *"everything's all right, I will love you always"* . . . I didn't want to do avant-garde experimental, free jazz music with people screaming about the futility of existence – I wanted to do pop music. But with words that are about what things are really like. You know, there's no way I'd write about cruising down a highway.'

Not in a Hillman Imp, that's for sure. In Jarvis' mind, Tom Wolfe made even the most mundane subjects seem exciting. 'He was a revelation. Reality wasn't this grey lump of concrete after all, and it's been my personal thing ever since to try and do that. To be specific. To look at the kind of thoughts people have when they're on the tube.'

Steve and Jarvis had also managed to make two more videos, one for Warp (The Aphex Twin's 'On'), and shame upon shame, Slipstream's moronic House anthem 'We Are Raving' for Island, which they accepted because Jarvis wanted some extra pocket money for Christmas. The video for 'Babies' was also a cause for celebration – Jarvis rated it the most successful and pleasurably easy video they ever made. Using visual signposts for each lyrical observation, the video employed two of Bob Stanley's friends to play the twin sisters, Sceaux Gardens Estate in Peckham for location shoots, and, somewhere in the mêlée, Jarvis' childhood cuddly gonk ('I like to get things that mean something to me personally into the videos if I possibly can') and a shopping trolley to whizz the camera around. They were rewarded with their first ever appearance on ITV's *The Chart Show*.

Just in case anyone was wondering if Jarvis fancied a career behind the camera, he pointed out that music was preferable to film-making. 'Music has a kind of spontaneity that film-making hasn't. My songs are all about real things that have happened to me, real people that I've known, just slightly embroidered. The truth has got a little bit of beauty to it.'

Truth and beauty – Pulp's old faithfuls were still around, even if you couldn't quite recognize them. Armed with confidence in their portrayal of both, the group returned to the studio in October and December to record new tracks for the next single. In a year when Pulp had secured a major deal as well as playing a live broadcast to the whole of France on a wet Parisian evening, things were ending on a thrillingly high note. For Jarvis, though, the year's most memorable experience was 'sexual activity in St Paul's Cathedral'. Finally, without irony or bitterness, Pulp could almost believe life could be so wonderful . . .

12

inside pop: a story in three years

Nineteen ninety-three began brightly with a January appearance on ITV's *The Beat*, premiering the forthcoming single 'Razzmatazz' alongside 'Sheffield Sex City' and 'Babies', a trip to France supporting Suede and, at long, long last, a new John Peel session, premiering three more new tracks, 'Pink Glove', 'You're A Nightmare' and 'Acrylic Afternoons'. 'If we do want to do a new album,' Russell quipped, 'Jarvis is going to have to get a new girlfriend and then we'll tell her to pack him in so we can get a new song. Then she can get back with him and he can write a song about that.'

In line with the press push, Jarvis was promoted to the front of the sleeve, while the others presented an unfocused backdrop. Released in February, 'Razzmatazz' was shaped from the same peaky, adrenalinized mould as 'Babies', with an equally virile, effortlessly anthemic chorus and a lyrical intro to beat all intros – *'the trouble with your brother . . . is he's always sleeping with your mother. And I heard your sister's missed her time again this month'*.

'Razzmatazz' was also notable for the fact that Jarvis' feelings toward the opposite sex weren't lamentful or regretful but more matter-of-fact and distanced, as he admonished someone for her vain attempts to handle her decidedly unsparkling life – (*'I saw you at the doctor's waiting for a test. You look like an heiress but your face is such a mess'*) – as she ended up alone watching TV with Milk Tray, and not a boyfriend, for company.

Not the kind of powders pop stars usually contemplate;
Jarvis on the threshold of being packaged, 1993
(Neil Cooper)

Jarvis reckoned 'Razzmatazz' was the most bitter song Pulp had ever done. But he was at pains to tell *Melody Maker*, 'However harsh I am about the people in "Razzmatazz", I'm not writing from above their level. I've got a lot of experience of being just as sad as them, if not more so.'

The B-side 'Inside Susan: A Story In Three Parts' was another third-person narrative. According to the sleevenote, the track would 'follow Susan from Rotherham puberty through wild teenage years in Sheffield to her eventual marriage and settling down somewhere on the outskirts of London'.

The first instalment, 'Stacks', was Pulp's most glam-pop-sounding song to date, sparsely arranged with handclaps and squidgy Moogs at the fore. Best of all, it owned surely the first rock'n'roll lyric about a trainer bra (sky-blue, underneath the crochet halter top). Part two, 'Inside Susan', lay a hypnotic groove under Jarvis' spoken tale of bus journeys and drunken parties, with the brilliant observation of a girl with *'a fire within, and all that stuff . . . it's just that nobody dared jump into her fire and risk being consumed. Instead they put her in a corner and let her heat up the room, warming their hands and backsides in front of her and then slagging her off around town.'*

'59 Lyndhurst Grove' was the finale, a throwback to the group's broody balladry, with Candida's solemn organ drone and Jarvis' strained croon, with a narrative inspired by a party Jarvis attended in the posher part of Camberwell, but with a theme of female dependency and dissatisfaction that stretched all the way back to 'Little Girl (With Blue Eyes)'. It turned out that Susan was a composite of two girls that Jarvis knew. He freely admitted that girlfriends in the past had hated being subject matter for his lyrics: 'They thought I was a bastard for writing about them, and I don't blame them. Especially when I wouldn't even tell them to their faces the things I was talking about in the songs.'

One girlfriend even used to hit him for the effrontery. 'You have to be fairly personal in your songs, otherwise it's just a load of rubbish, but there is a thin line between that and just reading out your diary,' he explained to *Melody Maker*. 'But I feel horribly guilty about that now.'

Jarvis and Steve had polished their videomaking technique by producing one for Tindersticks' single 'City Sickness' in August. Now it was the turn of 'Razzmatazz', which they had the bright idea of shooting at the world-famous cabaret the Moulin Rouge in Paris, while over in France for a show in Nantes supporting Suede. They were amazed that the club agreed, but less amazed when, on arrival, the owners changed their minds. An on-the-spot decision was made to film in their hotel bedroom (the Ideal, one of Jacques Brel's old hangouts, so the spiritual vibes were obviously right), adding footage of Jarvis lip-syncing in Paris' red light district, La Pigalle, and the band playing in London's salubrious Sunset Street club in Soho when they got back. The result, an encapsulation of seedy, faded, chintzy glamour, the Pulp way.

'Razzmatazz' was Pulp's third *Melody Maker* Single Of The Week in a row – a group could get used to this sort of acclaim. But the single also made the UK Top 100, peaking at 80, an achievement few would have believed within their grasp a year earlier. It was a good time to embark on their biggest UK tour yet, in support of St Etienne, whose 70s-into-90s synth-pop was a suitable foil for Pulp. John Best recalls that the shows were great, and gratefully received, with after-show gatherings enlivened by Jarvis playing Big Head, with a large papier-mâché head balanced on his shoulders (at other Pulp-related parties, the guests might play pass the parcel or other games explained in *Disco-Very*, like Pass The Matchbox, The Kissing Game, The Mattress Game and Animals).

Pulp spread the gospel wider via two major live events – the first ever Sound City festival in April, held in Sheffield, where the Pulp show was broadcast live on 1FM, and the Phoenix

Festival in July (where *NME* described them as: 'Suede stripped of pouting bombast'). The group premiered another new song, 'Lipgloss', which they had just recorded.

There was gloss everywhere you turned. Jarvis was a teasing, demonstrative, camp presence, a fashion *assailant*, with drip-dry deadpan comments from the stage and sartorial elegance off it. 'I don't own any casual clothes,' he once observed. 'You never know who you're going to bump into.' Pop stardom was evidently a duty: in *The Face* Jarvis admitted to being a pop star twenty-four hours a day. 'On call, like a doctor.'

On one side, he was flanked by Russell in a sharply cut, bright suit (lemon or lime being a favourite) and one of his hundred-plus pairs of sunglasses – he'd taken to wearing them because he didn't want to put people off with his stare-crazy eyes. When he took them off, he would invariably reveal glittery eyeshadow to match the suit. On Jarvis' other side was Steve, equally self-possessed and smart, with a line in bright ties. Just behind, Candida, usually in some stripy, though demure, blouse and skirt, while Nick was allowed to play in drummer-casual T-shirt and jeans.

With Pulp demoing in September and then returning to start recording a new album with Ed Buller, it was time for Island to play the game of Marketing The Band. The decision to release a compilation of the three Gift A- and B-sides on Island meant that the label and Fire had finally reached an agreement. Pulp records would now bear the Island imprint, and the new release could serve as both a boon to overseas markets who hadn't seen many of the Gift originals (it would be released in the UK, on a special mid-price, to thwart any costly imports) and a neat way to close that particular chapter.

With a cover photo shot in the heart of neon-lit Soho, *PulpIntro – The Gift Recordings* came out in October and made the Top 30 in the album charts. Reviews appeared everywhere – music press, teen press, national press, regional press, fanzine press – all positive. Pulp's chintzy glamour seemed universally applauded.

Released in October, 'Lipgloss' was Pulp's first Island-stamped single, and broke into the Top 50 chart. The track maintained the theme of 'Razzmatazz' with a glance at someone's failure to maintain her social skills and appeal in the face of male indifference: *'Though you knew there was no way it was gonna last for ever, it still shook you when he told you in a letter that he didn't want to see you.'* With its charged atmosphere, niggly guitar line and tack-sharp chorus, 'Lipgloss' was Pulp's fourth great single in a row. As Desmond Lynam would say, how *did* they do that?

It was unusual for a man to write from a woman's perspective, or to address his lyrics to women, but Jarvis had being doing it since 'Little Girl (With Blue Eyes)'. He thought it was something to do with his upbringing 'where there were no blokes around at all. So what I learnt about sex was from eavesdropping on my mother's friends having conversations in the kitchen, in the afternoon after I'd come home from school, 'cos you're curious when you're younger and you want to find out. All these snippets of information gave the female view. My mother had to teach me how to shave, which was funny because she'd never done it before.'

There were also the parties his mother and Auntie Mandy had held, 'where people snogged on the stairs, and stuff like that. That was my introduction to those kind of things.' Yet there were no stories of successful couplings, no happy endings. That Jarvis would never get married was an early vow – he couldn't see the point as no one he knew had stayed together. The husbands had all left, and the women were all left to cope.

Jarvis returned to the subject of Sheffield for the first 'Lipgloss' B-side. Despite some nifty jazzy undertones, 'Deep Fried In Kelvin' was more unfocused and rambling than Pulp's previous flouncy disco operettas, though Jarvis' dressing-down of Kelvin Flats, a particularly frightening Sheffield council estate – *'where the pigeons go to die'* – had its moments. 'You're A Nightmare' was a sweltering cabaret ballad with a mirror-ball chorus and a simple personal saga of sublime loathing.

Jarvis saw insecurities and weaknesses as well as strength and depth of character in the people around him – all potent material for his lyrics. Suburbia was a particular fascination for Brett Anderson and Damon Albarn too, but while Anderson writes about housewives on valium and Albarn depicts dull, routine lives, and people taking trains home from work to 'leafy nowhere', Cocker actually figures inside his own songs, writing in the first person singular, and actively *celebrates* what he sees.

Jarvis: 'Damon's more a detached observer of these things whereas our songs tend to spring from personal experience, and I get worked up. If you drive through suburban areas, you might think, "Oh look, all the houses are the same," and they are, but if you live there, you realize there are a lot of differences. Where I lived, there was a bloke just down the road who dressed as a man the top half and a woman on the bottom half, wearing pleated skirts, women's walking brogues and American tan tights, and there was my Uncle Ralph who lived across the road, who used to sit in his window with a German helmet on, listening to the Russian radio, playing his accordion, and more. Maybe because it is quite a bland and uninspiring place to live, people invent little lives for themselves. It's insulting to treat people as a mass.'

They came a little unstuck on the 'Lipgloss' video, though you could never have told from the finished, vividly colourful results. Being the first single on Island, it was big budget time, and the group decided to spend the dosh on the Eggopolis, a so-called 'inflatable environment' they had spotted in Liverpool one weekend. The problem was finding a studio large enough to hold it but Pinewood (next to the James Bond set) fitted the bill. Then the structure took too long to inflate, leaving time enough to film in only two of the four 'eggs'. Jarvis later contracted flu while editing the video in his sister's loft: 'It still makes me feel ill every time I watch it.'

With demos completed in Sheffield, Pulp entered London's Britannia Row Studios with Ed Buller to start work on a new album. They recorded intermittently between October and February 1994, only pausing for the odd radio and TV session and seasonal shows like another *Les Inrockuptibles* festival in France and a short headline tour. The band made its debut on 1FM's *Mark Radcliffe Show* (premiering 'Joyriders', 'Have You Seen Her Lately?' and 'His 'N' Hers' alongside 'Lipgloss'. Three days later, they tore through 'Lipgloss' on Channel 4's youth extravaganza/disaster *The Word*, where Pulp were ceremoniously introduced as the 'City Of Steel's bright new things'. Which was ironic, given Pulp's history, but at least it made them sound special.

Like 1992, 1993 ended on a string of highpoints. Jarvis still hadn't installed a phone in his house but Pulp were in the charts. In front of a crowd or the camera, every Pulp manoeuvre seemed to do no wrong, from Jarvis' wardrobe and beguiling stage ballet to the way each song was hammered home with a rousing chorus. When was the last time Pulp had faced a negative review? Jarvis had moved from his Camberwell council house to a smarter Ladbroke Grove flat, near Rough Trade's offices, an end-of-an-era statement in itself. In *NME*'s Top Singles of 1993, 'Lipgloss' made number six (Suede's 'Animal Nitrate' was top), an accolade rivalled, if not overtaken, by having 'Lipgloss' played on the hairdresser's radio on *Coronation Street* and one of *Emmerdale*'s characters talking about going to a Pulp concert in Leeds.

The only way was up, baby . . .

13

more sex, please, we're british

The album sessions continued through Christmas and were finished in February, just in time to allow more concerted press/radio promotion for the next single. Backed by two up-to-scratch, suburban-set, synth-simmering B-sides (the wistful, queasy 'Street Lites' and the giddy, queasy 'Babysitter', where Susan reappeared), 'Do You Remember The First Time?' was Pulp's fifth treasurable pop anthem in a row. Said Russell, 'I don't think we sat down to write hit singles, to approach things commercially, but more *artistically*. I find pop music more interesting and difficult to try and do than indie music.'

Jarvis was all itchy, frustrated envy again, though his lyric had a much more universal theme, that of losing your virginity. Jarvis recognized that the event held a monumental significance for people at the time but this faded away over the course of time. Incredibly, no one had framed the subject in a song before, but then no one else would have done it in quite the same touching and titillating way as Pulp. There was talk of vibrators – '*still, you bought a toy that can reach the places he never goes*' – alongside the memorably plaintive request – '*no, I don't care if you screw him, just as long as you save a piece for me*' – which would have sounded great on *Top Of The Pops*, if Pulp had been asked to appear. But the producers declined to ask, despite the single cracking the Top 50.

In the end, Pulp took themselves on to the television screens with another masterstroke of the imagination. Jarvis thought it was neat to make a short film about people's first sexual experiences as well as the usual promo video, and persuaded Island to finance the documentary.

In June 1993, Jarvis had made a cameo appearance as a conjurer, The Great Cockrini, in *Carrera*, produced by Steve Mackey, written and directed by their St Martin's chum, Martin Wallace, and broadcast by Channel 4. Now it was the trio's turn to use their post-grad skills for Pulp's benefit. But because the group were recording the album at the same time, they had to hand over pop-promo duties to Pedro Romani, who remains their first choice for video. (Interesting fact: two extras in the 'Do You Remember?' video were Johnny Dean and Chris Gentry, soon to form Menswear.)

The documentary had to be set up as easily as possible too. In the end, those interviewees Steve got to agree to appear – Vivian Stanshall, Pam Hogg, Jo Brand, Elastica's Justine Frischmann, Vic Reeves, Bob Mortimer, Terry Hall, John Peel, Alison Steadman and Candida's mum, actress Sandra Woe (interesting fact; Woe played the posh woman Hilda Ogden cleaned for in *Coronation Street*) – were filmed in a make-shift studio in Britannia Row (actually, the ping-pong room) when the guests could spare the time. This meant that the group had to down tools and shoot the action at odd moments but they managed to construct a twenty-six-minute epic about the myth and reality of deflowering that was touching, funny, revealing, silly, surreal . . . all those Pulp adjectives.

Linking these star comments was Jarvis' own admission of heavenly surrender – on that aforementioned patch of grass in Weston Park, Sheffield, just months short of his twentieth birthday. Both parties were virgins – 'Which meant that neither of us had to perform,' Jarvis was relieved to report. And they took all their clothes off: 'Something I've always been quite pleased about because it made it seem quite innocent and natural.' Given one word to sum it up, Jarvis said, 'Necessary.'

In the *NME*, the other Pulps confessed to their undoings,

which equally suited their characters. Candida lost hers to Peter Mansell, who was still her boyfriend; Russell to his friend's girlfriend by accident (he rolled onto the wrong girl), in a tent on holiday; Steve to a glamorous blonde, nine years his elder; and Nick in a loft conversion 'on some nice orange scatter cushions'.

The whole exercise was an extension of Jarvis' disbelief in happy endings. These were confessions of fumbling and farce rather than magic couplings with background strings. As he told the upmarket sex monthly *Ludus*, 'You tend to hear songs about love and stuff when you're growing which can give you a distorted impression of what love is really like. I think it's good to write songs that give a fairly deadpan, straight impression of things.'

'Do You Remember The First Time?' was released the same week in March as the documentary was premiered at London's Institute of Contemporary Arts. A month later, Pulp entered the album charts at number nine. Bona fide pop group stardom was theirs: the mountain had finally come to Mohammed.

As usual for a Pulp album, Jarvis' lyric sheet began with the plea, 'Please do not read the lyrics whilst listening to the recordings.' A quick perusal would tell you that Jarvis named the album *His 'N' Hers* because the songs addressed the relationship between boys and girls struggling with adolescent trauma, detailed in hysterical and miserable detail, and men and women struggling in a world of control and possession, freedom and dependency, the dream versus reality. If you take away the punchlines and funny fumblings, Jarvis was revealing the pain of the past; his lack of great role models when growing up was reflected by his own failures. To quote Morrissey, *'I can laugh about it now but at the time, it was terrible.'*

As Jarvis told *Melody Maker*, the underlying theme to *His 'N' Hers* 'is that thing where two people start wearing matching clothes, their personalities start to merge, they know exactly what each other's thinking, and they haven't a· whole personality of

Pulp enter their newly sartorial-elegant stage, 1994

(*Kevin Westenberg*)

their own any more. They've just got half of something else. And if that's taken away, they're less than a person.' How ironic that they finished the album on Valentine's Day.

The opening 'Joyriders' was, like 'Fairground', both a classic opener and a momentary detour from the Mills & Boon-erisms. The image of Jarvis' Hillman Imp breaking down on a Sheffield estate just across the way from marauding fourteen-year-old baggy ravers is both funny and tragic: *'Hey you in the Jesus sandals, do you want to come over here and watch some vandals smashing up someone's home?'* Being used to harassment, Jarvis feared the worst but the kids only forced him to listen to techno tapes in their stolen Ford Sierra while hot-wiring his car for him. A perfect state-of-the-nation address to an alternately bumpy and dreamy beat.

The sex wars began with 'Lipgloss', then climbed down a moral notch or two for the simmering adulterous storyline and cod-disco beat of 'Acrylic Afternoons', with Jarvis begging for a legover – *'on a pink quilted eiderdown, I want to pull your knickers down'* – while the adulteress's kids play in the road outside. (Interesting fact: the track opens with some atmospheric incidental music the group named 'The Tunes of Evil' but as soon as it was committed to tape, accidents started to happen: the mixing desk blew up, the multi-track tape of 'Joyriders' disintegrated, Ed Buller developed a bad back, and when the band decided to destroy the music, the engineer wiped the wrong track.)

The mid-tempo 'Have You Seen Her Lately?' was an adjunct to 'Lipgloss', but a more compassionate message to the girl, telling her she might still have time to escape: *'First you let him in your bed. Now he's moved inside your head . . . no, don't go round to see him tonite, he's already made such a mess of your life.'*

'Babies' paved the way for 'She's A Lady', the first disco-style track Pulp ever rehearsed, and the album's meeting place for Pulp old and new. The Brel-style melodic melodrama fuses with another liberal swipe from Gloria Gaynor's 'I Will Survive' (as the unreleased 'Live On' did) over Barry White rhythms, but the polished whole was much more than the sum of the parts. These sequencers were *slick*. Jarvis, meanwhile, lambasts the one who has abandoned him while being unfaithful himself with a certain lady – *'selling pictures of herself to German business men / well that's all she wants to do'*. Since Jarvis always stressed the autobiographical nature of his lyrics, did this incident happen to him or one of his friends, you wonder?

'Happy Endings' encapsulated Jarvis' preference for reality over dreams, though the glistening, overwrought Eurovision melody – Pulp play Abba – is the stuff romantic dreams are made of. 'Do You Remember The First Time?' was next, a why-not-me? storyline extended in part by 'Pink Glove'. The track got its name from one of Candida's pink gloves, inspiring Jarvis with an image of a woman holding on to her man by way of accessories and charms (like 'Lipgloss', except now it's baby-doll nighties and leather) and keeping him on tenterhooks. This was all to a class Euro-disco beat and expert grunting and whinnying from Jarvis: *'I know you're never going to be with me but if you try sometimes then maybe you could get it right first time.'*

'Someone Like The Moon' was a solemn, unsettling ballad with a familiar theme – a woman alone in a suburban day-mare, finding reality harder to accept than picturebook romance. The delivery is beautifully heartfelt, with a drama and pathos to rival Mike Leigh: *'The radio only plays love songs so she cries . . . in the evening it gets better and she thinks it's not right that someone so stupid can so easily screw up your life.'*

The album finale, 'David's Last Summer' (was this the same David from 'Babies'?) shows that practice really does make perfect. Here Pulp lay down a funky-cooking, slinky beat beneath Bri-Nylon strings, Russell's noodling guitar and Jarvis' spoken narrative. Like ABC and The Human League before them, Pulp had capitulated to the black beat but without selling their pasty-white Sheffield souls. The setting was a last, all-too-brief summer holiday (the opposite of Bobby Goldsboro's 'Summer (The First Time)'), featuring a bottle of cider, boating lakes, midnight swims and the end of the season. And carnal melodrama: '*Oh please stay for a while. I don't want to live in the cold.*'

His 'N' Hers was Pulp's true coming of age, a unique slice of scuffy magic realism. With its warm, dishevelled, school-disco, kitchen-sink (*not* kitsch-in-sync) appeal – Jarvis put it down to the fact that the group still couldn't play, 'but who's noticed?' he pointed out – the album could hold its own in a year dominated by Brit-pop landmarks like Suede's *Dog Man Star*, Blur's *Parklife* and Oasis' *Definitely Maybe*. The threads of glam, disco, New Romanticism and Euro-balladry had found a natural pattern, while the music's faded-glamour seediness and cabaret cheesiness were preserved by a ripening production and more assured playing skills. All in all, *His 'N' Hers* showed what Pulp could achieve with a few quid and a bit of pampering showered their way.

As for Jarvis, he finally learnt to write about his adolescence without naivety or embarassment – in other words, *His 'N' Hers* was the album *It* should have been. Ironically, in doing so he was mirroring his old rival, Morrissey. There was a similar outsider's view of the world, seen very internally, with a definite music-hall delivery of curdled camp and home truths. While neither had a political axe to grind, there was plenty of social comment on a decaying Britain with violence and insecurity at the heart of the culture, though Jarvis was clearly not lamenting things past. He *definitely* preferred the present. Oh, and he always wanted a shag. Moz-style celibacy wasn't quite his style . . .

It meant that Jarvis was good enough to stand comparison with timeless British pop narrators like The Kinks' Ray Davies, painting pictures both affectionate and sardonic of his country and its occupants, and playing masterfully with the colloquial aspect of British language. 'Cocker's skill is his listing prowess of place names no one else would use, of details no one else would notice, and people no one else would write about,' said *Select*.

Jarvis: 'I tend to use more events and things than what goes on in people's heads, not wishing to use adverbs if I possibly can because they nail an emotion to whatever action is happening. I prefer to describe the action, and properly, and let the emotional content come more from the music. Rather than "I stared at her wistfully", or "I sat in the chair wistfully". I'd love to have adverbs phased out of the language.'

Peter Dalton nails it on the head when he says, 'Jarvis has a unique talent in that he is able to articulate experiences that make the listener go, 'yeah!', with recognition. He has that wry or sardonic edge that makes it work. I'd call it "verbalizing the *Zeitgeist*".'

Of course, had he spoken like Prince Charles, or even in cockney, it wouldn't have sounded remotely funny or astute, but armed with that deadpan, sanguine Sheffield delivery, everything he said sounded plausible and comical.

Plausibility was an aim, but fantasy wasn't out of the picture. Jarvis had always liked airbrush work, and had used an illustration by Philip Castle (who had done the original poster for *A Clockwork Orange* and album sleeves for bands like Mott The Hoople) for the sleeve of 'Do You Remember The First Time?' With a decent budget, they were able to commission Castle to paint an airbrush of the group, which cost £4000 (incidentally, at the time of writing, no one had bought the original). 'The reason airbrushes appealed to me was that they could make things look better than they really were.' Magic realism, in other words, with an Athena stamp of quality.

Philip Castle: 'I think Jarvis and Steve felt that the look of my work enhanced what they were doing. What they'd seen and liked was the hairstyle pictures in my first book – they were all very muted, in browns and hardly any colours – and they wanted something similar for the album sleeve.'

Island wanted to quickly follow the album's success with another sure-fire single and reissue 'Babies'. Pulp initially resisted

The photo that Philip Castle airbrushed into the *His 'N' Hers* **sleeve, 1994**
(*Kevin Westenberg*)

but eventually agreed, though they insisted on using the original mix rather than a remix, plus there would be three new tracks for value-for-money purposes. Housed in another of Philip Castle's 'hairstyle' airbrushes, *The Sisters EP* was released in May, and this time cracked the Top 20, bringing Pulp their long-awaited *Top Of The Pops* appearance. Bona fide pop stardom, one step nearer . . .

The three new tracks had been recorded during the *His 'N' Hers* session. 'Your Sister's Clothes' carried on the 'Babies' storyline, four years on, as the younger sister gets her revenge over one of Candida's best fairground-swirling synth lines. (Interesting fact: the track was originally titled 'Glass' because the group thought the music sounded like the American minimalist composer Philip Glass, introduced to the others by Mark Webber.) 'Seconds' seemed to sum up the whole Cocker universe – *'sometimes second best is all you're going to get'* – while suggesting that second best was better than boring old perfect best anyway. To support the theory, 'Seconds' sounded like a ragbag of other Pulp songs with nothing much new to offer. The fourth track, the six-minute 'His 'N' Hers', investigated the world of endowment plans and figurines in what was surely a musical tribute to 70s disco-pop champs Hot Chocolate, with percolating, bubblegum synths and a chewy funk bassline that got progressively hotter as Jarvis did, panting, *'It looks so good but does it turn you on?'*

Which was a question cultural commentators had started asking about Jarvis Cocker. Since he had added heavy-breathing to his extensive repertoire of top vocal turns and begun writing about knicker-ripping lust, Jarvis' application to the Sex God club had been accepted. The press picked up not just on his androgynous skinniness but his fashion-assailant mobility: the *Observer* magazine put him on the cover and rapped rapturously over his 'knee-length fake fur coat, tartan scarf, tweedish jacket with leather detail, oil-slinky-purple shirt, burgundy needle-cords, pointed stack heeled banana hued cowboy boots and plastic rimmed glasses'. Slowly but surely, the ironic sex nerd was turning into a real sex symbol. Ziggy Stardust in a tweed jacket. The thinking woman's crumpet. Pop's Angus Deayton.

Russell: 'For me, the sex-symbol stuff is relatively recent since I first knew Jarvis as this gangly lad in short trousers, a speccy, spotty git whom women thought was a joke. Somehow, and I don't quite know how, he has transformed himself. The first person I ever knew that actually fancied Jarvis, which was only about six years ago, was my Auntie Val. She just said, "Jarvis, you're sexy" and I thought she was joking. Almost all of the band have lived with Jarvis at different points, and shared beds with him, so the thought that he could be conceived of as sexy is bizarre. But what was once a ridiculous idea has become an accomplished fact.'

Jarvis' sex-symbol status was more the debonair, cheeky kind, more Roger Moore's raising of an eyebrow, than the exposed hirsuteness of Sean Connery. The kind of sex symbol that mums, and Auntie Vals, can appreciate as much as teenies and fashion snobs.

Russell: 'I think he does very well not to take that sex symbol stuff too seriously, and knows that it isn't 'cos of him but just a part of showbusiness. But he's certainly cut out for it. In fact, it's the only thing he is cut out for 'cos little things like getting across London and stuff like that seem to present him with enormous difficulty. But he's a brilliant performer on stage and can think of different lines every night, which I've aways admired in him. Whenever anybody else thought he was a bit of a tit, I thought he was a great performer.'

Mr Sex-On-A-Stick views all the attention with the requisite irony. 'I was very aware that I wasn't a sex symbol when I was a seventeen year old. Everybody wants to look presentable but people who think that they're sexy have got problems. But I'd be lying if I didn't say I was pleased because for so long I wasn't considered good looking, though I find it quite strange. I can't say I feel more sexually confident but I am more confident as a person because I feel like I've been given a seal of approval, which makes me less anxious about myself. Though to be honest, the only parts about myself that I'm happy with are my hands, which is why I move them about so much.'

Kate Moss' anorexic beauty had become the icon of female fashion but the male model world had followed the gay male ideal of sculpted muscles. Jarvis represented another option, a scrawny but self-assured sexiness, underpinned with a dose of androgyny.

'I always thought the muscle image was a bit weird anyway, as all the girls that I knew didn't fancy big muscly blokes,' he ponders. He told *The Face* that the thick-set, pit-bull, crop-haired look of the male model world wasn't a good way for a man to look. Why not? 'Being skinny is neater and tidier, and it's not got bulges all over,' he elaborates. 'If women were all thin, and men were all muscly, it would be like two different species, like a horse having it off with a tiger.'

He couldn't change his spindly body dimensions but in the facial department, Jarvis could switch between a Michael Caine-style decent squareness and a contact lens job exposing those sharp cheekbones and fluttery eyes. You'd think he might do away with the glasses altogether in a fit of vanity but the National Health frames have remained. As we know, some ladies find glasses sexy but Jarvis' motives are anything but devious.

'I wore lenses when I first came to London but always found them irritating, like I had something in my eye. Which, of course, I had. The thing that finally put an end to it was when I stayed at Steve's one night and put the lenses in the lids of two herb jars overnight, then put one in in the morning. It immediately started burning, because I'd put it in the cayenne pepper lid, so it'd marinated overnight. I went to Moorfields Eye Hospital, which told me contact lenses weren't any good for my eyes anyway, and I had scars beneath my eye lids from wearing them. So I was told to only wear them on stage. I can get away with it for just an hour or two – if I wear glasses, they tend to fall off or droop, which is never the coolest thing for a stage performance.'

The whole package – the sex symbol, the 70s threads, the pop-tune genius – had come together very well. Suede and Brett Anderson retained their appeal but they had proved a tad too grandiose for the kind of lads who went for Oasis. Jarvis found himself just behind Blur's Damon Albarn in the league of pop coolness and magazine interest. Melissa Thompson at Savage & Best was now having to fend off press interest, live shows were almost all selling out, and the business shackles of the past had been cast off. Where to go next? Onto TV.

Appearing on the hallowed *Top Of The Pops* was still a necessity for Bona Fide Pop Stardom status, which Pulp finally won when *The Sisters EP* broke the Top 20. 'Being on *Top Of The Pops* was the fulfilment of a lifetime's ambition,' Jarvis told *Vox*. 'Like a lot of people, I suppose, you grow up watching it and practising and hoping. In our case, being in the band for a decade, we'd thought about it a lot . . .'

That week, the BBC were filming the show live, so during a swift mime of 'Babies', Jarvis took the cameras by surprise by flashing open his jacket to reveal the words 'I Hate Wet Wet Wet' written on the inside. The Wets had been number one for umpteen weeks, and Jarvis wanted to make known his opinion of their horrible homogeneous fake soul. (Jarvis also made known his love of Whigfield's 'Saturday Night', as, aside from the wonderfully dumb simplicity of the song, the single stopped the Wets' 'Love Is All Around' from equalling Bryan Adams' sixteen weeks at number one.) Wet Wet Wet vocalist Marti Pellow made his annoyance known as well, though his threat of physical retaliation had to be a joke.

Jarvis: 'I heard the show was going to go out live, and I thought that if I didn't do something to surprise the powers that be, even if it meant we were banned from the show for all time, I'd never forgive myself. They all thought it was quite funny, actually.'

Obviously impressed, BBC's *Pop Quiz* invited Jarvis onto the 14 June show two weeks later, where he teamed up with then teen-star Chesney Hawkes and soul siren Des'Ree, against Marcella Detroit (ex-Shakespears Sister), Toby Jepson of heavy metal Brits Little Angels and Patric from teen-fancies Worlds Apart. Introduced as 'a mixture of Scott Walker, Morrissey and Quentin Crisp', the boy soon shone, showing expertise in Hot Chocolate's lyrics and on The Human League, and then famously answering every quick-fire question in the last round to take his team to victory (47 to 34).

The music press made mountains out of this sterling performance; it was generally felt, as Jarvis did himself, that he had struck a blow for 'our side' against the mainstream. 'I remember being completely pissed,' Jarvis owned up. 'Wiping the floor with the opposition was somehow important to me as I was sick of people letting you down on shows like that, being crap and boring. Pop music is not Arts Council-funded or something you think ought to exist, it's part of popular culture. People choose to have it in their homes, it gets all mixed up with their lives, so it becomes more than just music. You can do that by talking on TV just as well as writing songs, but usually the personalities on TV are so bad, they turn you off. TV presenters are like irritating, hyperactive children who insist on pushing their face into the camera, which isn't my idea of entertainment. If you can be OK, which I consider myself to be, then it can be good.'

Unsurprisingly, Fire had been keeping tabs on the rising tide of Jarvmania. The label had already released *Freaks* on CD, and followed this with *It* in the autumn. (Interesting fact: *It* had already appeared after a bankrupt Red Rhino had sold the back catalogue to Cherry Red label, which released the album, adding 'Looking For Life', 'Everybody's Problem' and 'There Was'. But Tony Perrin and Pulp owned the rights, so Cherry Red had to withdraw. Fire's version only has 'Looking For Life' tagged on, although it still lists all ten tracks, presumably because Clive Solomon didn't want to pay for new artwork.) It was a timely re-release because the very first cover version of a Pulp track, 'Wishful Thinking' from *It*, had been put out as a single by new London girl duo Golden, on Bob Stanley's Icerink label. This more electro-pop version suited the melody better, and the girls' voices suited the words better than Jarvis'.

Solomon subsequently gathered together the first four Pulp EPs to make a Fire version of *PulpIntro*, under the title *Masters Of The Universe*. He didn't see anything underhand in his actions. 'The back catalogue sells steadily but we haven't heavily re-promoted it – you don't see big adverts, do you? Why? I've got a history of getting slagged off for everything I do around Pulp so maybe I didn't feel ready to take the abuse that might be coming . . . anyway, it was a mixture of reasons. I assume Pulp don't want to see their records repromoted so perhaps that's also why I've held back. But there's an awful lot of money to be made if I do. I released the compilation because the music's good, and I signed Pulp because I loved them, so the record is as much for me as anyone else.'

Pulp were notified about the compilation, and Jarvis agreed to write sleevenotes for it if 'Silence' could be left off. Rightly or wrongly, he took the opportunity to share his contempt for the label, by way of referring to his original sleevenotes for 'Tunnel' (the B-side of 'They Suffocate At Night') from 1987: 'I first entered the tunnel on the 10th July 1985 . . . that was fifteen weeks ago and guess what? I'm lost . . . I walk for about eight hours a day but I've still never seen a glimmer of light that would tell me I'm nearing the end of the tunnel . . .' Years later, he now added, he had discovered that Pulp's first contract with Fire was dated 10 July 1985: 'Had my unconscious mind been trying to tell me something?' he added.

Solomon refused to print Jarvis' words and replaced them with his own. 'I thought they were very cynical, and rightly or wrongly, I took offence at the very negative inferences about Fire. Basically, it was a bit much. He can express his opinion at any time but here, he had the chance to be constructive.' Jarvis angrily claimed that he couldn't understand what the fuss was all about, and in retaliation, refused to help with the reissue of *It*.

There were bigger and better things to think about. Pulp played the British summer festival circuit – Glastonbury, the first T In The Park in Glasgow, and Reading – all of which were televised. The 'Do You Remember The First Time?' documentary had been shown on Channel 4 (as part of their *Late Licence* programme) in July; the group had performed an acoustic version of 'Babies' on BBC2's *The Late Show*. Then came the Mercury Music Prize in September, when *His 'N' Hers* was one of the ten finalists up for the £25,000 award.

After each album had been introduced in turn, Jarvis' speech was a simple rendition of John Miles' marvellously mawkish 70s anthem 'Music': '*Music was my first love and it will be my last / Music of the future and music of the past,*' and so on. Yet it wasn't enough; the voting panel cast five votes for Pulp and five for M People. Panel chairman Simon Frith had the final vote and chose to side with M People. Members of Pulp were heard to boo from their table. 'We need the money, they don't,' said Jarvis after. 'My money would have gone to charity anyway as I buy all my clothes in Oxfam.'

Pulp then headed off for their first American dates, supporting Blur. They covered 10,000 miles and played eight concerts. Pulp felt the San Francisco show was special as fans turned up with old Pulp artefacts to sign but Jarvis remained sceptical. 'If you start thinking about how you're going to break America, you end up breaking yourself. The tour driver was on his seventh wife but that doesn't mean Pulp will start writing about American weirdness. We could write songs about being on the road but I think we'll leave that to others.'

The groups returned to play Aston Villa Leisure Centre and London's Alexandra Palace (where Jarvis' first words on stage were: 'This is a special evening . . . it's the start of something . . . or the end of something. One question though – are there any M People fans here tonight?'). Blur were naturally getting a lot of attention but Pulp won their fair share; every flick of the wrist and hip elicited untold numbers of screams. If people didn't know what they were about before the exposure to Pulp in concert, they would have cottoned on that day. Did anyone in the UK under twenty-five have an excuse for not knowing who Jarvis Cocker or Pulp were?

Even more so after 19 October. In a year of TV and radio profiles, the jewel in the crown had to be Jarvis compering *Top Of The Pops*. Not just playing on it but *compering*. Producer Rick Blaxill had rescued the show from obsoletion by bringing in various celebs to present it, and Jarvis had become his favourite pop star. And so it came to pass that Jarvis entertained millions of impressionable viewers, and made an indelible impression. The land of mainstream dummies had once again been invaded by 'our kind'. This is what we want our pop stars to be like. But Jarvis wasn't just a pop star, he was a *multi-media celebrity* . . .

Jarvis: 'Like meeting Geoff Travis, and *Pop Quiz*, presenting *Top Of The Pops* felt like a turning point for me. Take That were number one with "Sure", so I said at the end that "Take That *are Top Of The Pops*", which Rick Blaxill liked, and he made everybody else say it afterwards. I know Jimmy Savile probably did it first but I revived it. But don't get me wrong, I'm not forging a career here. I'm not that bothered. I just do something if it's worth doing – or if it's paid well enough.'

Two weeks after Jarvis' *Top Of The Pops* triumph, Pulp appeared on Channel 4's *Live At The Lighthouse* special, which raised money for AIDS sufferers. As at Alexandra Palace, they played two new tracks, 'Common People' and 'Underwear', which showed Pulp were rising to the songwriting challenge.

Nineteen-ninety-four's gala year on TV ended with some choice we're-here landmarks. They were invited to play the launch party for Quentin Tarantino's now legendary *Pulp Fiction* at London's Ministry Of Sound. Jarvis was more than happy to be associated with the American producer: 'He's aware of the insignificance of everything, which is why I like him. People get lines from television all the time, they litter your head. It's the closest you'll get in films to what people say in real life.'

Pulp also appeared at the annual Prince's Trust Gala Concert, held at London's vast Docklands Arena, the first time Pulp had been involved with matters of state since they claimed social security. Phil Collins was on the same bill, a man Jarvis had called 'anti-music'. Pulp performed 'Babies', sex scenario and all, but nevertheless, it transpired that Prince William was a Pulp fan. What could top that? Maybe the *Observer* magazine front cover, or what about a Christmas show at the Theatre Royal, Drury Lane, enlivened by tiny star lights at the back and an equally glittery staircase for Jarvis to descend, in the best showbusiness tradition. 'I do suffer from vertigo, so every time I get on this staircase, you'll know I'm really giving something,' he said. The stamping of tiny dancing feet caused large cracks to appear in the Grand Circle balcony.

'It is always good to bring the house down but perhaps not quite so literally,' Jarvis said afterwards, always good for a spontaneous quip. The management couldn't prevent Pulp from doing an encore but banned them from the venue. A small price to pay for a live milestone.

The group treated the show as a bit of an end-of-era statement too, with versions of 'Love Is Blind', 'Death Comes To Town' and 'I Want You' among the already vintage *His 'N' Hers* tracks. 'Jarvis is quite touchy about some of those old songs as they represent a different Jarvis, don't they?' Steve confided. 'They're quite painful because they represent the worst time of his whole life when he was fucked up, by girls, or a girl. It is Jarvis as a virgin, looking to jump into the swimming pool of life. *Freaks* is when he's jumped in and he's stuck in a relationship and it's all wrong, everything he thought would happen isn't. *Separations* is getting out of that and then *His 'N' Hers* is looking back on relationships.'

Hillman Imp or not, Jarvis and Pulp were driving carefree down pop's corridors of power with no brakes . . .

14

last night a minimalist american composer changed my life

Jarvis: 'Life is a plastic bag – it's empty at birth and then you fill it as you wish during mortal years. Sometimes it gets too cluttered and you have to empty it out. Some stuff can get stuck at the bottom where you can't get at it, so it's important to carry around what you really need.'

At the beginning of 1993, Jarvis had reminisced about how, at the start of the 90s, things had started to go on an upward slope for Pulp. 'Even though it may have been a very small gradient and you wouldn't have bothered to put a warning sign on it,' he reckoned. In case anyone was mistaken, 1995 was an alarmingly steep, tumultuous, almost vertical leap, with 'careful – low oxygen' signposted on the way.

It started as early as the first week in January, when the *Daily Star* pop page ran an excited 'What is Jarvis Like?' feature and knighted him 'pop's sexiest nerd'. Was there any greater compliment? Another sign of mainstream crossover was being asked to present the award for Best Female Artist (to Eddie Reader) at the Brit Awards in February. During the course of the night, he found himself standing at the urinal, next to Tom Jones, a similar crooner and stage craftsman. When two sex symbols collide . . .

Otherwise, the group kept their heads down, writing, rehearsing and then recording through to April, though after recording with Ed Buller for three years, the group and Geoff Travis reckoned it was a good idea to move on, and move up in the producing world.

As with *Freaks* and *Separations*, Pulp grew to dwell on the mistakes of *His 'N' Hers* more than its achievements. Steve: 'Ed was the right choice at the time but the album didn't sound quite right. At the time, Geoff Travis and Nigel Coxson said it sounded really reverby and echoey, and it's true, but at the time we thought it sounded fabulous, so you can't blame Ed. We were still considering him for the next album, as we thought he would have learnt from his mistakes, and better the devil you know, and that we could steer him away from that, but then Suede released *Dog Man Star* which sounded even more reverby than anything before, so we said no way.'

At Geoff Travis' suggestion, the band listened to the work of Chris Thomas. 'One of the best producers in the known universe,' according to Travis. Thomas had got his lucky break working on Roxy Music's epochal second album *For Your Pleasure* (Bryan Ferry hadn't liked the original sessions and so called on engineer Thomas to step into the breach). Pulp definitely shared something with Roxy – a quirky, retro-futurist feel, with a mesh of wildly varying styles, simultaneously electronic, rock and pop – 'the synths and the squishy bits,' thought Geoff Travis – so the connection seemed well founded. Thomas had worked with wildly varying acts too, The Sex Pistols, The Pretenders and Elton John among them, but Pulp still considered a number of other choices.

Steve: 'In late 1994, me and Jarvis had this concept, to make an LP that was twelve pop songs and every one could be a single. We even talked about getting Benny from Abba to produce it, or Mickey Most, pure pop producers.' AOR expert Alan Tarney, who had worked with acts like A-Ha and Cliff Richard, was considered, as was Stephen Hague. 'We liked his work with Pet Shop Boys but he was very cold and lacking in soul when we met him,' Steve remembered.

Steve subsequently make a tape of all four producers' work, four songs each, which he gave to each member. 'Of Chris' work, I put on Roxy Music's "Love Is The Drug", The Sex Pistols' "Holidays In The Sun", The Pretenders' "Brass In Pocket" and a John Cale track, and it was so obvious that his stuff stood out. We gave him a demo of "Common People" from a Peel Session and he really liked it, and he proved great to work with too.'

In turn, Chris Thomas was madly enthusiastic, saying that Pulp didn't remind him of anyone except Roxy Music. 'They've got highly individual ideas and that's as important as being great musicians,' he responded.

It took a whole week in the studio to nail 'Common People'. As Steve recalls, 'We had forty-eight tracks of music, with something on every track. We'd always wanted the song to have the same chugging sound as ELO's "Mr Blue Sky", where you don't hear all the different instruments but just this wodge of sound, epic but not bombastic. We had four days to mix, and on day four, it got to five o'clock, and all we could hear was a wall of noise. Then Chris did what turned out to be a classic move which set the standard for the album, which was to change the mood. We were slightly shy of each other, as Chris can be a bit intimidating at first, but he came back with a bottle of Remy, which the three of us drank, and three hours later we'd finished. Jarvis put this acoustic guitar on top, and that was it, and it sounded fantastic.

'Me and Jarvis sat in my basement and played it about five times, thinking it was really good, that it definitely didn't sound like a record anyone had made before. Six months before, we'd been listening to a lot of minimalist music like Steve Reich, La Monte Young and Glen Branca, which Mark started us off on, having got into them through Jason of Spacemen 3. These composers were all conceptualists, so we had this concept of there being only three chords in the whole song, to start off quiet and end up with this huge wall of sound, as if it went up a mountain, and be louder than anything we'd ever heard. It changed a bit in

Pulp enlist some new members, 1995

(*Lawrence Watson*)

the studio but it did achieve that as well, and remained a pop record. It had a minimalist feel, with drones, like a single C that holds for the whole verse, plus it had what I thought were the best lyrics Jarvis had ever written.'

'Common People' found Jarvis backtracking again, but only as far as London, 1989. Despite his own efforts and the media's fondness for caricature, Jarvis wasn't solely sex-centric, his beady eyes casting through London's fields of revelation. He admits that the most telling reaction he experienced on leaving Sheffield was that, contrary to his beliefs, the class system really did exist.

Jarvis: 'Before I left Sheffield, I thought maybe the whole world was like that. You're living in a certain situation and you haven't got any perspective, so I never understood before. Most people in Sheffield are kind of in the same boat, though of course there are posher and rougher areas. My area, around Intake, is now one of the roughest in the city but in my time it was all right, far enough away from The Manor, one of the worst estates. But as soon as I moved away, I suddenly realized class did exist 'cos you meet people from different backgrounds, and I began to socialize with people who'd been to public school. I hope I never got too much of a chip on my shoulder about it but it used to irritate me that I knew there were people in Sheffield whose lives were going nowhere, like mine had been, but who were quite talented and intelligent. They had been fucked up because there was no oppor- tunity to do anything creative or interesting while there were people in London who were idiots in quite good jobs, making lots of money. And I got a bit resentful about that sometimes. But I was never one who'd only drink in pubs that served Tetley Bitter, or wore a flat cap.'

The realization was, in fact, a true turning point. 'Suddenly you had to think about everything again, and what was important to you, and how you saw things. That was what made the band really. Gave us material.'

The motivation behind such an essential track as 'Common

Jarvis reads up on marriage etiquette, 1995
(*Valerie Phillips*)

People' had come about in an ironically nonchalant manner. 'It was daft, really. Me and Steve had a bit of a practice round my home, and we came up with this anthemic sound, aiming for something like "Life Is Life", and he said "Fanfare For The Common Man" or something, that crap song that Emerson, Lake & Palmer did, which I thought was funny because 'common' is an insult, isn't it? That interested me in doing something that was about common people, but in the way that it is seen as an insult rather than, say, Paul Young's "Love Of The Common People", which is more about the idea that there *is* such a thing as a common person, like "these noble savages".

'As soon as the title was there, then I thought, "oh good", and immediately remembered this Greek girl I met at St Martin's. She did believe in common people, having come from a rich background, and she thought of the lower classes as something quite exotic, and something she could go and see as a tourist, to go to Hackney, to take something from it and use it in her own work. But I don't believe that "common people" exist, and that it's a daft way to think.' Jarvis told her so too: that she could rent a shitty flat and go to rough pubs but had a get-out clause because of her money. 'I told her she wasn't trapped like they are. Anyway, she wouldn't have it.'

Neither did she have Jarvis either. He took a bit of an artistic licence in the lyrics and slightly embroidered the truth. 'No, she never wanted to sleep with me, unfortunately. She never actually said, as the song does, *'I want to sleep with common people like you.'* It was funny, though, 'cos when I moved to London, my Northern accent gave me this air of slight earthiness, which is the first time I was seen that way.'

Class-based story though it was, there was a sexual *frisson* underlining the song. 'I only knew her for about three weeks, on this sculpture course, so I never got to know her very well. I didn't even know her name! I just remember talking to her in the pub, and quite fancying her, but I didn't approve of her, and sometimes that's quite interesting, isn't it? Sometimes a bit of tension can add some spice to a relationship. That's something I've known from eavesdropping on my mother because I remember this bloke she was going out with one time, we used to go on little holidays with him, and I overheard her talking about him with a friend, and she said, "Oh, he's too nice." That's why she finished with him, 'cos it kind of irritated her, which was funny to think about when you're young.'

Once Pulp had finished the track, there was one slight hitch. Island thought 'Common People' was not only good, but too good, and wanted to hold it back and release it just before the new album in September.

Steve: 'We just said it has to come out now. There was an exciting mood in the air, which subsequently became Britpop – Blur's "Boys & Girls" was out, so was "Live Forever"; and "Common People" felt like a song of the moment. We were totally convinced, and Geoff Travis was right behind us, so we made Island release it.'

A release date of 22 May was set but the group were suddenly thrown back into the public eye when they got asked, at the last minute, to support Oasis at Sheffield Arena. Pulp had already been offered the slot but dallied too long over whether they should headline their next hometown show, so the offer went to The Verve. But then Verve guitarist Nick McCabe broke his finger (in a clash with security in France) and the band were forced to cancel. A commitment-free Pulp accepted the offer – at three o'clock on the day of the show . . . 22 April.

At least it left them with no time to get nervous. 'It was originally meant to be a secret and it certainly turned out that way,' Russell noted. 'It was a surprise to the audience but it was just as much of a surprise to us.'

The mass abandon that greeted Jarvis' appearance on stage was proof enough of Pulp's new level of popularity. Then came the release of 'Common People', which even now sounds as awesome as it did then. The instrumentation and arrangement was leagues ahead of previous Pulp tracks, the intended escalating force had been captured, and Jarvis' lyric was biting, funny, sarcastic, indignant: '*I said, "Pretend you've got no money." She just laughed and said, "Oh you're so funny." I said, "Yeah? Well I can't see anyone else smiling in here."*'

More than just a sly satire, this was serious. '*You'll never live like common people, you'll never do what common people do, you'll never fail like common people, you'll never watch your life slide out of view, and dance and drink and screw 'cos there's nothing else to do . . . you are amazed that they exist and they burn so bright whilst you can only wonder why.*'

The more gentle, soulful B-side, 'Underwear', returned to the bedroom: it's that moment when you get down to your underwear but the moment has passed, and you have to retreat. At the same time, Jarvis adopted the role of envious outsider, half way between friend and voyeur: '*I'd give my whole life just to see it, stood there only in your underwear.*'

Despite its colossal strengths, few expected 'Common People' to enter the chart at number two. If it wasn't for ITV soap-series *Soldier, Soldier* duo Robson & Jerome's 'Unchained Melody'/ 'White Cliffs Of Dover', then in its third week at the top (now the biggest selling single of the decade), 'Common People' would have charted at number one. The single sold 70,000 copies in its first week, usually enough to hit the top spot. More glory was experienced the next week when 'Common People' stayed at number two, while Michael and Janet Jackson's long-awaited new single 'Scream' went in at three. 'Jacko can spend his eight million pounds on his video for all the good it does him,' Jarvis observed. 'But I suppose it means we will never get invited to Neverland to have a spin on his big wheel.'

Was Jarvis startled by the song's chart-storming success? 'I thought it would do well – it's an anthem, isn't it? But it was a genuine surprise. The 1FM chart rundown was coming live from

Birmingham, with every band miming to their songs, which was exciting, so we travelled down in a minibus but had to wait in the leisure centre forecourt for about three hours. We had no idea when we would go on stage because we had no idea what position the single had got to. It was nervewracking. Around 5.30, I put my contact lenses in, and hadn't rinsed them properly, so my eyes went bright red, and then when we did go on, I fell over. It had been raining, so the stage was all puddles. This was supposedly our finest hour, and when the song goes loud, I jumped off the monitor, and slipped when I came down. I embarrassed myself in front of 10,000 people watching, with a giant video screen, so everyone saw it. But that's symbolic – in your moment of triumph, there's something that brings you down to earth.'

The press reaction was fantastic, from Single Of The Week in *NME* and *Melody Maker* to *The Times*' suggestion that the song combined 'theatrical flair with sly social commentary and a sure populist touch'. The *Guardian*'s view was: 'There are always going to be records that transcend personal taste and achieve a kind of grand consensual splendour. "Common People" is one of those records.'

With 'Common People', Pulp joined a select élite of British pop groups that not only released a string of singles that maintained a palpable quality but who made an emphatically unforgettable statement that created something more than just a pop song, and at the same time catapulted the group into another league altogether. The Jam did it with 'Down In The Tube Station At Midnight' and then 'Going Underground', The Specials did it with 'Ghost Town', and Pulp had now managed it with 'Common People'. Oasis might have shifted up a gear with 'Live Forever' as Blur did with 'Boys & Girls', but it couldn't compare. Even The Stone Roses and Happy Mondays had never managed such an iconoclastic single.

Timing, they say, is everything. As *Time Out* put it, 'It's the song that turned Jarvis Cocker into something of a modern folk-singer – ambassador for the misunderstood working classes, bubble-burster to rich bohemians everywhere.' Having been out of fashion for so long, Pulp were at last in line with the times. 'Even if it's only for a short while, it feels great,' Jarvis grinned.

Those in critical, literary circles were equally impressed. The late 60s playwright Joe Orton once said, 'You've only got to be sitting on a bus and you'll hear the most stylized lines.' These were now filtering down through the pen of Jarvis, with his unnerving accuracy – a fact noted by a *Guardian* feature on British pop's new scribes. 'Common People' was lauded as the best example of the new literary renaissance and Jarvis compared to Elvis Costello. Jarvis used to get the comparison because of the glasses (he even impersonated Costello, circa 1978's *This Year's Model* album, for *NME*'s 1994 Christmas issue) but now it was for what the *Guardian* saw as similar class-revengeful tendencies (not forgetting the sex-nerd similarities, and the fact that 'Common People' was set at art college among the chattering classes, as was Costello's '(I Don't Want To Go To) Chelsea').

Such accolades and attention could have gone to anyone's head, but as Jarvis observed, 'The good thing about success, though, is that, whereas I just used to think about me all the time, now I'm too busy with the band.'

The mainstream courting of Jarvis continued. Jarvis appeared on ITV's *Richard And Judy Show*, where the fans pressed up against the glass doors announced Pulp's transition to teenybop status. Channel 4's *The Big Breakfast* even had a 'Jarvis day'. The new *Top Of The Pops* magazine put him and Kylie Minogue on the front cover, and got them to interview each other. It seemed that nothing could upset the group's endless summer of praise.

Yet the unrelenting focus on Jarvis the Sex God and Poet Laureate was bound to be to the detriment of the other members' contributions, as well as to his own personal privacy – no celebrity can control the desire which he or she generates. For a while, Jarvis was safe. As he told *Select*, 'There's not much

Jarvis salutes the mainstream – with Richard and Judy
(*Liverpool Daily Post*)

scandal in my life. I suppose you can get caught shagging somebody you're not supposed to. But that wouldn't be much of a scandal because I'm perceived to write about that kind of thing anyway.'

He was right, because Jarvis was more or less congratulated by *Melody Maker* when, in a front cover feature, he was spotted 'in a quiet corner of a Menswear after-show party with a gorgeous young girl, legs akimbo, facing him on his lap, her skirt around her waist, his crotch against hers, the pair, oblivious to the drinking/drugging hordes, thrusting and grunting like extras from *Confessions Of a Britpop Idol*.' At the same time, the article made reference to the fact that Jarvis had a live-in girlfriend Sarah 'who may or may not be the saucy girly from the Menswear party.'

Worse was to come when, a week later, in another *Daily Star* pop page special, under the headline 'Pulp Friction' the 'daddy long-legs of pop that has become the Nineties' most unlikely sex symbol was spotted at an Oasis after-show party, having sex in front of gob-smacked revellers'. Jarvis' quoted reply was a perfunctory, 'I can't recall anything like that happening at all.'

It wasn't Jarvis' style to grope in public, let alone have sex in public, and the press have been known to exaggerate. Once or twice. Still gentlemanly in his conduct with the press and extremely careful to keep his relationship with Sarah out of public view (she apparently worked in a mental health centre, where Jarvis had once DJed, playing lots of Madness singles), Jarvis was unaware of the attention the article would get and subsequently felt betrayed, but ultimately powerless.

The *Daily Star* followed this titbit with the news that Jarvis was the next pop star to fulfil a long-held dream of becoming a screen star, by acting in, and directing a film co-written with Steve. In the apparently 'psychedelic movie' Jarvis is to play a Northern layabout who buys a rusty Ford Cortina and drives to London, according to the paper. Jarvis has, on several occasions, refuted the idea. 'I can't act, so that'd soon put a stop to anything like that. You wouldn't want to end up like Sting, would you?'

It was true, though, that Jarvis took to the catwalk, wearing a pair of pale-blue, pearly loafers with transparent toes. The occasion was the Pagan Fun Wear fashion show organized by producer/musician Brian Eno on behalf of the Bosnian aid charity War Child, where celebs offered items for sale. Jarvis' shoes, designed by second year college student Cecelia Vanman from the Cordwainers' College Of Shoe Design, fetched the most money of all the offerings, an impressive £5100. Jarvis took to the catwalk with a walking stick, feigning old age, or maybe it was his feet playing up after all these years. Maybe it was a metaphor for the crippling effect of fame. Maybe it was just plain daft.

Out of the press eye for now, the main focus was back on the new album. Sessions took place at the Town House studios in London. Chris Thomas had two engineers and a programmer to

Best foot forward: Jarvis at the Pagan Fun Wear Fashion Show, 1995
(*Piers Allardyce/SIN*)

Jarvis takes note of a Common Person, Glastonbury, 1995
(*Steve Double/SIN*)

assist him, which meant less work for the band (should Candida need to play a different keyboard sound, the technicians were able to alter what she had already recorded, which she admits left her feeling less involved). At Thomas' suggestion, they worked on each track separately rather than record each instrument in turn. Things progressed well, only for fate to interrupt them again with more fantastic luck.

Anticipation over The Stone Roses' headlining set at the Glastonbury festival on the Saturday night had reached fever pitch – it was to be their first UK date in five years – when guitarist John Squires broke his collarbone and shoulder blade after falling off his mountain bike in America. A replacement group was quickly sought, but who could do the job without it being a letdown? It could only be . . .

Pulp had played Glastonbury in 1994 but to return as headliners on the festival's twenty-fifth anniversary was a major coup. It was a long way from the first time Jarvis attended the festival in 1985, when he and his girlfriend screamed at each other all weekend, and went home early. Rather than drive back and forth from a Bristol hotel, the group elected to stay in tents with the common people. 'This way, we can have more fun,' said Jarvis, plus the benefits of the backstage area, with creature comforts like flushing loos and a bar.

The group now had plenty of time to get nervous, but Jarvis approached the Saturday like any other day. That is, any day spent walking around teeming thousands inside an adult version of a child's playpen. He refused the offer of a security guard out of embarrassment, and wandered around freely among the pierced multitudes before sitting in his tent for three hours for what he called, 'my own mini-healing festival. I centred myself.' It didn't work. 'I was crapping myself. It was the most nervous I'd ever been before a concert. I remember, ten minutes before we went on, I held on to the sides of the chair as tight as I could, as I was convinced I would have an accident and break my hand or something, and wouldn't be able to go on. But once we did, it was great. I don't believe in fate as such, but in this instance, it just seemed like fate.'

It was also fate that saw Pulp debut a new song, 'Sorted For E's And Wizz', that the group had finished just two weeks earlier, with a lyrical theme located in the world of drugs and festivals and raves, although the doleful melody wasn't the kind of song to make Glastonbury dance their heads off. That was left to 'Common People', which they sang last; the song's true effect could be gauged when a field of 50,000-plus jumped up and down, singing along to every word, as Pulp strung out the end section in classic rock-anthem style. 'Take it *down*,' Jarvis instructed the others, like Bono would do. *Well*. As the song ended and the crowd cheers grew deafening, Jarvis left the stage, saying, with unusually direct sincerity, 'Thank you for making this a very special night for us. I hope it was special for you as well. Hope you enjoy the rest of your time here. Glastonbury, twenty-five years. Here's to twenty-five more, all right.'

There were more triumphs to come. Pulp sold out Sheffield City Hall, in front of a fanatical home crowd, before headlining the Leeds Heineken Festival in front of a Glastonbury-sized gathering. Suzanne Catty was right – Jarvis was to the stadium manner born. During both festival appearances, every karate-kick, arse-twist and wrist-flick was a matter of celebration, for both the audience who saw in Jarvis a jack-the-lad spirit they could easily emulate, and for Jarvis, who had finally made it into orbit after all this time.

15

sorted for hits and controversy

It transpired that Island's argument against releasing 'Common People' in May was that Pulp wouldn't be able to write a follow-up song to match. The fact that Island had felt that 'Common People' was too good to release months before the single had seriously upset the group.

Steve: 'Island thought we'd sell bucketloads of the album on the back of "Common People". We were quite annoyed that they had a lack of faith in us, as if we'd write eleven songs that were inferior. "Common People" might be the best song on the LP but we had to write another twelve to fifteen songs and couldn't have that attitude.'

The band's writing bursts in late 1994 and early 1995 had produced 'Common People', 'Underwear', 'Pencil Skirt' and 'Monday Morning', with the rest deemed unsalvageable. Steve remembers the buzz of 'Common People' encouraging them like nothing else, and they ended up crammed into a room and writing the rest of the album in under two weeks. As Suzanne Catty had noticed, 'When Jarvis and Candida, especially, put their heads together, they come up with some amazing stuff, and quickly. I've seen them rehearse on a Monday and by Wednesday have seven songs ready and record them in four days.'

Jarvis was just as quick on the word front. Two nights before Pulp were demoing the tracks, Jarvis wrote all the remaining lyrics. 'He might have a slight theme and a few catchphrases but he always writes lyrics the night before he has to sing them,' Steve explained.

Pulp frantically finished the album through Britain's long hot summer. With the prospect of diving into press and radio promotion immediately after, Jarvis managed a week's holiday, choosing Iceland of all places. 'I know the heat this summer was good in a way but I got sick of it after a bit, especially in London, and it was getting me down while we were making our album, so I wondered where would be cooler, and thought ice was cool, so I picked Iceland. There weren't many people there either. We just hired a jeep and drove to volcanoes and bathed in thermal springs, which smelt a bit eggy 'cos it's all sulphur, isn't it? But once you got used to that, it was all right. Stuff did cross my mind every now and again but I just tried to have a holiday, the same as anyone would do, and not think of being in a group.'

He even got to stay in Björk's house. 'I had met her on *Top Of The Pops*, and asked her where I should go, and she was going to be away, so just offered. So it wasn't like a showbizzy thing.'

On his return, Pulp went straight into promotional mode, both in the UK and Europe. Between the press interviews, they grabbed an afternoon to film a version of 'Disco 2000', one of the forthcoming album tracks and a proposed single, for a November edition of *The Jack Dee Show*. The group's twenty-four-hour-a-day aesthetic was clear from the rehearsal – they pull all their usual stage moves, Jarvis twirling around and ending the song crouched, his legs folded up under him like a deckchair. Before they settled down in the dressing room to watch *Coronation Street*, waiting for the stage call, Jarvis talked of his holiday, and the price of fame.

'It's just that it eats into your free time, which is quite a strain. I wish I could have allotted a bit more of my time on the dole to now but I don't complain that much 'cos at that time, I really wanted something to happen, so it would be silly to say you didn't want it any more.'

The downside of wanting to be wanted is that you can no longer control where and when it happens – the Menswear party incident, for example. 'Well, it is a bit of a nuisance if you commit some impropriety in some private place, and then it gets reported. I'm quite a reserved person anyway, you see, so I like the idea of getting carried away, and it doesn't happen that often, so I wouldn't want to have to censor myself and be sensible and worry if there was a photographer there to snap me in a state of undress. And you have to keep giving your opinion all the time, don't you? You get asked about things. I do like to give my opinion, yeah, not that I think it's particularly great, but it's mine. That's part of the reason people join bands, I'd say, because they're show-offs and want people to take notice of them, so . . . I can't complain.'

Fencing with the press is accepted as a necessary evil, but it was more the personal details that mattered. 'At this very moment, my sister's come down for the weekend and I would have gone to the train station to meet her but I've had to get some-one else to do it, so you have to make an effort to arrange things that, before, were quite easy. I haven't seen her for a long time, and people are always asking you to do more, and sometimes you have to do more 'cos it is important not to lose all your friends.'

As Jarvis knew as well as anyone, pop wasn't just about the music, it was everything else around it. But with the release of the new album, attention could at last be diverted back toward the music. Without it, Jarvis' popathon would be like 'a car without petrol', as the singer put it.

September came around, and the first proof of the new record-ing sessions was unleashed. Pulp had wanted the brilliantly titled 'Sorted For E's And Wizz' as a single. 'On a simplistic level, we wanted to get off the pattern of doing uptempo singles, as we'd done seven stomping songs,' Steve said, 'but it would have been a commercial risk as radio doesn't like smaller records.' And so a compromise was made: a double A-side with 'Sorted' and 'Mis-Shapes'.

This wasn't to denigrate the latter. The best way to follow up a thrilling anthem like 'Common People' was to produce another, and 'Mis-Shapes' was almost as good, with an equally identifiable theme, a clarion call that exemplified the bond between Jarvis and his audience. Jarvis could still easily remember his Sheffield adolescence, as he and his fellow 'freaks' ran the gauntlet against the townies on a Friday night. As he explained, 'Those people do hunt in packs, but the misfits or mis-shapes, because of the fact that they're more individualistic, are easier targets, so the idea of "Mis-Shapes" was the fancy that the misfits would form some kind of an alliance, or army, and take over.'

The term 'mis-shapes', he added, 'was derived from the chocolates that get rejected because they're not up to scratch, but still taste as good as the ones that get in the boxes of Milk Tray, so they get put into bags and sold cheap. I thought some people are like that.'

Jarvis' lyric is unexpectedly, deliciously sneery. *'Now we can't help but see the future you have mapped out is nothing much to shout about'* he counters, and then gets nastier when he casts a withering look at 'common people' culture, such as that populist institution, the National Lottery. *'What's the point of being rich if you can't think what to do with it / 'cos you're so bleedin' thick.'* But the central crux of the lyric is positive and gleeful: *'Brothers, sisters, can't you see, the future's owned by you and me. There won't be fighting in the streets. They think they've got us beat but revenge is gonna be so sweet . . . we won't use guns, we won't use bombs, we'll use the one thing we've got more of, that's our minds.'*

Two editions of the single were released in September. The 'Mis-Shapes' single included 'P.T.A. (Parent Teacher Association)', with more let's-get-naked sentiments over Pulp's most Northern-soulful excursion yet, and the Glastonbury version of 'Common People'. The 'Sorted' single settled for an additional two mixes of 'Common People'. A video for 'Sorted' was cobbled together from footage from the Glastonbury Festival (Jarvis

Now we are six . . . Pulp shot during the 'Mis-Shapes' video
with Mark Webber in the ranks
(Rankin)

strums an acoustic guitar – hey, protest singer!) while in the video for 'Mis-Shapes', Jarvis even risked a spot of acting by playing a nightclub compere, an oik who throws a drink over the nerd, and the nerd who ends up machine-gunning down the oiks. Jarvis, the unexpected socially and sexually desired victor! Yes, revenge is going to be so sweet.

Jarvis: 'It would be nice, wouldn't it? The same stuff is still going on, though probably not as much as then, but I got some letters from people saying it was the same in their town, where you still have to run the gauntlet on a Friday night.'

This time, Island anticipated the single entering the charts at number one; advance orders were a massive 180,000, Island's biggest ever, more than U2 ever achieved. Yet the single went in at number two again, held off by Simply Red's 'Fairground', understandably so as this was Simply Red's first release since the zillion-selling *Stars* album.

'Sorted For E's And Wizz' was commercially overshadowed by 'Mis-Shapes' but the former spectacularly got its own back by engineering the first Pulp controversy on a tabloid-headline scale. Well, the subject was drugs, so what did you expect?

Steve and Jarvis had both felt the social as well as the musical potential in the original Acid House movement but the disillusionment had soon set in for both of them. It's not often that you think life will change for the better, and when it doesn't, the disappointment can last for a lifetime.

Steve: 'We realized that nothing had changed and all the same divisions came back. I remember taking E at a Sunrise gig, where people were nice to us all night, and then it was seven in the morning and we realized we were in the middle of some field, trying to hitch a lift, with thousands of cars going past and no one would stop for us.'

Jarvis had the same recollection: 'People were saying, "Nice one, man. Empathy," all night, but I lost my friends and I tried to get a lift home and nobody would help. Even if it was all drug-induced, I really thought it was the start of a big change in people's attitudes, people being friendly while they were out rather than wanting to have a scrap. I thought it would seep into the rest of people's lives, that if you're nice to people, life is more fun, but it isn't.'

The expression 'Sorted For E's And Wizz' had come from a girlfriend of Jarvis' in Sheffield who had attended The Stone Roses' Spike Island extravaganza 'where all she could remember was a load of dodgy blokes walking around, saying, "Is everyone sorted for E's and wizz?" But it could have been any festival.'

The empty rhetoric many experienced during those days was brilliantly nailed in Jarvis' lyric: *'And this hollow feeling grows and grows and grows and grows, and you want to phone your mother* and say, *"Mother, I can never come home again 'cos I seem to have left a very important part of my brain somewhere, somewhere in a field in Hampshire."'* Put together with a downbeat melody, shaped by some clipped, Moogy funk and the coming-down ache in Jarvis' voice, the effect was sublime. It was the reality rather than the dream. As Jarvis suggested, ' "Sorted" isn't the kind of song you'd want to hear if you were off your face.'

He knew the subject matter would prevent the song getting daytime airplay or children's TV rotation but he hoped its intended anti-drugs message meant it wouldn't get banned. The song wasn't banned; just the sleeve, believe it or not, due to its various mock-ups of a paper wrap to hold speed (wizz) in, with origami instructions on how to make your own.

With Britpop starting to peak, stars like Damon Albarn, the Gallagher brothers Noel and Liam and our man Jarvis were as fair game as any Hollywood or Brit-TV celebrity.

When the *Daily Mirror* assimilated the information, coming soon after the news that seventeen-year-old schoolboy Daniel Ashton had become the fifty-first person to die of taking Ecstasy, the newspaper went into moral overdrive. On 20 September the cover headline ran 'BAN THIS SICK STUNT' followed by the words 'Chart stars sell CD with DIY kids' drugs guide'.

In Jarvis' mind, he had been blatantly misinterpreted. He was adamant that he was stressing the fact that – for some people anyway – no matter how great a time you have on drugs, the artificial nature of the experience hung around, like a ghost. 'It's that empty hollowness you feel in the morning when you do something like that, when you feel your brain won't recover, and the only knowledge that survives is that you don't feel very well.'

Not wishing to be misinterpreted as encouraging drug use, Pulp agreed to withdraw the sleeve. The following day, when the lead headline was the Pulp-tastic 'LET-OFF FOR SEX SHAME JUDGE', the *Mirror* ran a small front page inset under the headline 'PULPED BY THE MIRROR', claiming it had 'scored a major victory' with a reader's poll voting 2112 to 770 to ban the record. The Association of Chief Police Officers, drug support groups and even Shadow Home Secretary Jack Straw had called the sleeve irresponsible.

At heart, the *Mirror* was reacting more against the sleeve than the song and printed Jarvis' press statement and a portion of the lyrics alongside the by-line: 'HAUNTING: Pulp's lyrics reflect Cocker's anti-drug message.'

The incident recalled nothing so much as the *Sun*'s overkill surrounding The Smiths' 'Suffer Little Children' (the B-side to 'Heaven Knows I'm Miserable Now') in 1983, when outrage was expressed over what was interpreted to be sick exploitation of the most horrifying murder case the country had ever witnessed, rather than what was Morrissey's sorrowful lamentation for childhood's end.

In an interview with the *Mirror*, Jarvis claimed that he didn't want this sleeve to obscure the record's message, but maintained that the sleeve design was nothing to do with him or the group, 'no matter how flippant that may sound', and that he had seen the finished design 'but didn't take much notice of it at the time because it didn't offend me'.

His excuse wasn't flippant, just weak. The original sleeve was to be in the shape of a wrap itself, which proved impractical, but since Jarvis had observed, 'The song was about drugs so the sleeve should have something to do with it', it was pointless acting innocent. The act was prolonged when he concluded, 'These days, the only thing I do for kicks is ride my bike.'

Jarvis' avowed taste for alcohol argues a case against straight-edge living – but the fact that the tabloids cast Jarvis as a villain probably made him a bit more of a hero in the eyes of Pulp fans.

He even owned up to enjoying the controversy a bit. 'I think it's pretty cool that pop stars are actually front page news now.

Cut-out for the top – pulp figures for the *Different Class*
album cover and tour
(*Rankin*)

A few years ago that would have been unthinkable. The best thing is that we didn't go looking for trouble. It's not outrage for the sake of it, which I hate.'

It was time to put the troubles behind them and get on with the business of the new album. The finishing touch was the album artwork, which came smartly embossed in silver and included six double-sided cards with scenes representing the twelve songs on the record, enabling the buyer to choose his or her own front cover. Classy. Now a permanent feature of the group, having played and contributed to the songwriting process on the record, Mark Webber made his debut on the artwork too, in the shape of a stand-up cardboard cut-out alongside the other five members, which the designer then placed in numerous bland, domestic settings (for example, in a bedroom or a greasy-spoon café) that clearly suggested serious bouts of alienation.

But there were now six instead of five cut-outs – Mark Webber had been made an official member, and had played and contributed to the collective songwriting process on the album. 'Last summer, they had a big meeting,' he told *Q*. 'They gave me this once-in-a-lifetime offer. I was flattered and shocked. They didn't have to do it.'

Jarvis chose to call the album *Different Class* 'for two reasons. The first being flippant. It's a phrase in Sheffield that describes something good, like "top class" or something, but there is the fact that a lot of the subject matter is me coming to London, which was the first time I found out I was from a different class, so the title seemed appropriate.'

His 'N' Hers was the summation of a period in Jarvis and Pulp's life, and he had decided the subject matter of the new album should be different to its predecessor. 'Otherwise I couldn't see the point. I still wanted to retain a personal feel as it would have been terrible to go into mouthing off loads of platitudes about subjects I didn't know about, like reading an article in the *Guardian* and then trying to write about Bosnia, as you're not going to get much insight into situations. But I did want to broaden my scope a bit so I tended to look to my own experiences since moving to London and draw on that, then try and see the social things that were represented in my life, i.e. the things that had happened to me, like "Common People".'

Steve: 'We had the idea that this album was about the class issue, as we all came from quite working class backgrounds, but had moved into this different world, and all the false values it exhibits, while all the relationships on this record are as disappointing as on previous ones. I don't think Jarvis has moved on in that sense. "Something's Changed" is a love song but that was written ten years ago, just after *It*. Take that away and it's not very optimistic about man versus woman. It's realistic.'

Sex was hardly likely to disappear off Jarvis' agenda but in the final reckoning, he thought that there was a better balance on the album. 'Probably a more realistic portrayal of how much of my time sex takes up, which is about a third of my life. The rest of the time, I'm asleep.'

Jarvis reckoned three songs dealt with sex but there were definitely six that revolved around the subject. 'Mis-Shapes', which kicked the album off, wasn't one of them, but the slinky, sweet 'Pencil Skirt' was. Jarvis had gone down on paper as owning an acquired adolescent taste for pencil-skirted ladies, and the usual frustrated lust is clear from the first breath: '*When you raise your pencil skirt like a veil before my eyes / like the look upon his face as he's zipping up his flies.*' As it turns out, Jarvis is under the bed, and simply waiting his turn: '*I'll be around when he's not in town / I'll show you how you're doing it wrong.*'

If Island feared Pulp couldn't match 'Common People', then what did the label think of the equally anthemic and twice-as-ambitious 'I Spy'? Coming straight after the single, the track unfolded with a shimmering, spoken passage which soon gave way to a more uptempo section, with Russell's violin and a Romany flavouring more pronounced than any track since *Separations*. More importantly, there was a real orchestra careering alongside the group just as in Scott Walker's heyday. At last! The track then cut back to another slow, dramatic interlude, before building up to a rallying 'la-la-la' singalong and a final dreamy, expansive coda.

'I Spy' was as lyrically advanced as the music. Jarvis squeezed in an early mention of '*I will survive*' but it's an ironic aside as the words are as negative, twisted, and gloriously bitter as Mike Leigh's misanthropic epic *Naked*, and the nasty side of the 'Common People' coin. The protagonist leaves the North for London and participates in a have vs. have not war of the classes, shagging a rich man's wife and promising to rescue her from upper-class ennui: '*You see I spy for a living and I specialize in revenge, on taking the things I know will cause you pain. I can't help it, I was dragged up.*

My favourite parks are car parks. Grass is something you smoke. Birds are something you shag. Take your Year In Provence *and shove it up your ass.'*

Revenge, served sour . . . ' "I Spy" is one of the most savage songs that I've ever written,' Jarvis concluded. 'It's definitely the most vindictive.' He dreamt it up remembering his time in Sheffield, on the dole, despising his surroundings. 'There you are, walking down the street, and everyone just thinks you're this useless, jobless piece of crap. But inside, you feel really strong. Their hatred sort of helps you feel that way. You know what's going on, you've got their number, and you know that you're gonna get your own back one day.'

'Disco 2000' is pure escapism afterwards, the strongest reminder of Pulp's *His 'N' Hers* pop blueprint, an outrageously catchy, camp glam-rock stomp with the most obvious steals from 70s pop iconography – the boot-stamp of Elton John's 'Saturday Night's Alright For Fighting', T.Rex's glitter-star guitar, Abba's sweeping gait and a huge swipe from Laura Branigan's HiNRG classic 'Gloria' (Deborah's name was initially Gloria but they were advised to change it, or pay royalties as Elastica had done to the Stranglers over 'Waking Up'). Jarvis recalls growing up alongside Deborah who gets it on with the other boys and then gets on with her life while Jarv remains a bit of a useless knob. The song ends with a resigned: *'Oh what are you doing Sunday, baby? . . . You can even bring your baby.'*

But why 'Disco 2000'? So that, just as Prince would make a mint when radios worldwide played '1999' in the year of its title, Pulp would clean up at the turn of the century.

'Live Bed Show' was a gorgeous, swaying ballad with a classically melancholic melody located somewhere between Jacques Brel and Abba. (Interesting fact: one set of chord changes mirrors an old David Bowie track, 'Cygnet Committee'.) Recalling the scenarios of 'Lipgloss' and 'Razzmatazz', Jarvis regards a woman's loss, as she lies alone in bed: *'Something beautiful left town and she doesn't even know its name. Now every night she plays a sad game. Called nothing's going wrong.'*

Though Jarvis admitted to liking strong-minded women, 'the kind who don't do what they're told,' why didn't he ever write about any? Was it because he never experienced any at close hand? The only time women triumph – such as Deborah in 'Disco 2000' – is when they don't wait around for Jarvis.

Side Two began with 'Something's Changed', an echo of an older Pulp, which indeed it was, as its wistful, 60s-tinged melody was written over ten years earlier, with new lyrics and a lilting orchestral arrangement that would have satisfied Burt Bacharach. The song stands as Jarvis' first contented love song, about the role of serendipity. Jarvis hadn't sounded this innocent and naive since the *It* album: *'Just give us a kiss to celebrate here today.'* But then Jarvis has always believed in love at first sight. Betcha he never expected it to happen though.

'Sorted' was a bit of a rude comedown from this optimism, then 'F.E.E.L.I.N.G. C.A.L.L.E.D. L.O.V.E.' elaborated further on the former's slow, eerie funk tract, with added bursts of stabbing, staccato beats (Jarvis even reckoned the track had Jungle influences). Lyrically, he was feeling more optimistic again, though he was keen to highlight the reality behind the myth of chocolate-box love: *'It's dirtier than that, like some small animal that only comes out at night.'* Recalling 'Something's Changed', he asked, *'Why me? Why you? Why here? Why now?'*. He also paused to ask that time-honoured question: *'What is this thing that is happening to me?'* It's just caught in your zip, Jarvis.

'Underwear' got its clothes off and on again fast before 'Monday Morning' echoed territory covered by 'Countdown', as a boredom-struck Jarvis is unable to foresee a future: *'Why live in the world when you can live in your head?'* he asks himself. *'Is this the light of a new day dawning? A future bright that you can walk in? No, it's just another Monday morning.'* It seemed a strange place for Jarvis to visit, given the way everything had escalated for him, but obviously memories don't fade that fast. The hint of ska in the music was an even stranger place to visit, but Pulp simply can't put a musical foot wrong.

In the closing 'Bar Italia', memories – in fact, any mental processes – don't stand much of a chance, not in Soho's famous late-late cappuccino hang-out, full of tired clubbers and small animals that only come out at night. After the kind of night you've had, and the kind of album Pulp have just created, there's a feeling of happy exhaustion in the air – you're fading fast, but you're not dead yet, so two sugars please. *'You can't go home and go to bed because it hasn't worn off yet and now it's morning. There's only one place we can go. It's round the corner in Soho. Where other broken people go.'* The album started with mis-shapes, and ends in the same place.

As fine as *His 'N' Hers* was, *Different Class* was in a class of its own. Pulp's endearingly awkward edge had been superseded by a lush polish but without losing any of the group's spirit. Musically and lyrically, they had moved from the local fleapit to Cinemascope vision, making a record as flamboyant and ambitious as Suede's *Dog Man Star*; both records also shared a love for, and a gladness to escape from, the suburbs. As *His 'N' Hers* was to *It*, so *Different Class* was to *Freaks* and *Separations*, the album where Jarvis finally nailed his stories and feelings of loneliness, resentment, and self-belief with that winning touch of magic realism.

It was important to note that, by talking about class, Jarvis wasn't turning into a politician. His inspiration came from personal incidents, not the need to make a point. What's more, Jarvis wasn't taking sides. The Greek girl was wrong to treat people as a demographic mass, but while Jarvis felt humiliated and revengeful in 'Common People', 'Mis-shapes' and 'I Spy', he could still see the conceits that were ingrained in the class structure, from all sides – the vain thoughtlessness of the upper class, the jealous insecurities of the middle class and the inverted snobbery of the working class, and none felt like home to him. Nor did Sheffield, where he was never accepted, though his roots are there.

Without exception, the previews and reviews of the album were unanimous raves. 'Their best album by a comfortable distance,' said the *NME*. 'Not so much the jewel in Britpop's crown, more like the single solitary band who validate the whole sorry enterprise.'

Different Class sold a staggering 301,000 copies in its first week, more than Blur's *The Great Escape* and not far behind Oasis' *(What's The Story) Morning Glory*, the fastest selling album since Michael Jackson's *Bad* eight years earlier. The media may have been exploiting the ever-escalating Blur vs. Oasis 'Battle Of The Bands' but Pulp were up there too, glad to be out of the ludicrous staged fight.

Jarvis even got to 'referee' the Blur vs. Oasis battle when he was asked back to compere *Top Of The Pops* the week that either Blur's 'Country House' or Oasis' 'Roll With It' would be number one. He excelled again, introducing Expansion with, 'Let me tell you about this next group – well, not a lot 'cos I don't know anything about them, but they're all the rage in the clubs.' He praised Diana Ross for influencing many people – 'Michael Jackson's plastic surgeon for a start' – and brightened up the chart rundown with 'Love to, darling,' after Corona's 'Try Me Out'. He was cheeky, he was flirty, he was the people's favourite . . . and then he finished with his best cheesy Jimmy Savile, telling the audience that, in the Blur/Oasis wars: 'You're the winners out there, 'cos you're getting a lot of good music.'

Between the release of the 'Mis-Shapes'/'Sorted' single and *Different Class*, Pulp completed a UK tour. Sell-out signs were posted everywhere, with just one little problem – those interfering tabloids again.

Jarvis had already seen the lighter side of Tabloid News when he played alongside members of Gene, Shed Seven and

Blur at a charity soccer match the previous week. At one point, a Wonderbra-less woman streaked on to the pitch, and headed straight for Jarvis, and for all the sad stupidity of the circumstances, the resulting photo had its merit, with Jarvis' bemused, faintly embarrassed expression set against the streaker's bouncing glee. But the night of 8 October was far more than harmless fun. Pulp were playing Cambridge Corn Exchange, when, before the show, a teenager approached Russell in the backstage area, asked if he did drugs, and offered him a wrap of speed. Russell declined the offer, at which point he was asked if he would pass the drug on to Jarvis. He declined again, and when the kid asked what hotel Pulp were staying in and what pseudonym Jarvis was under, Russell suddenly caught on, and turned around to see a zoom-lens-packing photographer standing in a doorway.

A similar incident occurred after Pulp's London show, when a hotel employee tried to make out that a member of Pulp had dropped some drugs out of their bag. What a kind Samaritan.

'It must have been a tabloid trying to set the group up,' Pulp's long-suffering press officer Melissa Thompson reckoned. 'They wanted a picture of Russell accepting drugs to make it look like, "Pulp foist drugs onto children". They can turn things round when it suits them.'

As they careered around the country, the legitimate media cavalcade was at it again. 'Jarvis Cocker grapples with fame' on the front cover of the *Guardian Weekend* magazine; Jarvis a guest on BBC2's kids' agony-aunt slot *Dear Dilemma*; Jarvis on Radio 4's *Loose Ends*; Jarvis visiting John Peel for a discussion of all things Pulp past and present, when Peel played their first session from 1981 and new tracks from *Different Class*. In their early days, Peel had liked Pulp enough to offer them a session; now he was claiming that 'Sorted For E's And Wizz' was a candidate for Single Of 1995, and contributed a voiceover to the national TV ad campaign for *Different Class*.

Pulp's appeal was always wide, and it was no surprise to see the group accepted equally on the teen-pop front when they played the *Smash Hits* Pollwinners' party in early December, despite Jarvis being voted Least Fanciable Male and Worst Dressed Person. (At last! Some negative press!) Of much more worrying dimensions was yet another tabloid intrusion into Jarvis' private life when, on 28 November, the *Mail On Sunday* ran a double-page spread under the headline, 'I WALKED OUT ON MY TEEN IDOL SON . . . WILL HE EVER FORGIVE ME?' Two journalists had tracked down Jarvis' father, Mack, to Australia, where he was recovering from a bout of alcoholism, broadcasting on a local radio station in Darwin, and about to release a CD of his own music. In the article, Mack talked of returning home when his son was thirteen, and noticing that Jarvis 'could hold a tune at a very early age'. Over the years, he had kept tabs on Jarvis' progress, but only from afar, through videos and magazines.

Jarvis' mother, Christine, surprisingly agreed to be interviewed, perhaps needing to vent her spleen. She claimed Mack was a good father but a lousy husband, whose cheques always bounced. Jarvis sensibly refused to comment, and hoped the story would go away as quickly as it had come. Just like the hysterical case of two representatives from Brighton Police Licensing Unit who confiscated copies of *Attitude* magazine from the Out! gay and lesbian bookshop in Brighton, after seeing them in the window, because the cover headline publicizing an interview with Jarvis read 'Cocker gets Cocky', which they deemed to be an offensive and indecent use of language. The head of the police unit admitted his guys had made a mistake.

Was controversy to follow Pulp and Jarvis at every turn? Almost as if they foresaw the problem, having released two singles with heavyweight themes, Pulp's last single of 1995 was 'Disco 2000', the album's poppiest, most carefree moment. Thus the word 'woodchip' finally made its debut not only in a pop song but in the singles chart too, where the song debuted at number seven at the start of December. The single came in two different versions, the first with various remixes, including one by Alan Tarney, the second with an extended version of 'Live Bed Show' and the new 'Ansaphone', where Jarvis worries that he is leaving messages for a girl who is too busy getting it on with another guy. Unlucky, this Jarvis fellow . . .

Not that the controversies were to abate quite yet. Before Christmas, huge flyposter ads started appearing around London with a photo of Leah Betts, the eighteen-year-old who had recently died after drinking too much water while on Ecstasy, with the word 'SORTED' beside her photo. The small byline at the bottom of the poster read, 'It took just one Ecstasy tablet to kill Leah Betts.' Would it be too paranoid to imagine that the group was being criticized for 'legitimizing' the word in the language of yoof culture?

If any confirmation that Pulp were considered a danger to society was needed, the fact that the police searched hundreds of fans as they attended the group's show at Bridlington Spa after the local council had initially attempted to have the show cancelled was it. A band spokesman said: 'They [the police] were just picking people up, left, right and centre, putting them in vans and taking them to the police station. God knows how many people missed the show because of it.'

In the end, the police arrested fifteen people for possession of soft drugs, and let them go with a caution. Maybe the powers that be reckoned Pulp fans would be planning to take masses of Ecstasy at a mid-week show.

At the same time, tabloid stories linked the group with the suicide of a sixteen-year-old, Jessica O'Riordan, who jumped out of a hotel window in Bournemouth on 18 December.

If 1994 had ended spectacularly, then Pulp could never have imagined how they would see out 1995. There were pathetic tabloid reactions on one hand, a half hour BBC2 special *No Sleep Till Sheffield* on the group broadcast on 18 December, where

Jarvis' mother and grandmother also chipped in comments (well, it was the least they deserved for they support they gave the fledgling group on the coal-scuttle and sticky-paper front). To top it all, the group announced an arena tour in March 1996 – their own arena tour. Those who once witnessed Pulp at the Sheffield Limit or Leadmill, the Hallamshire or the Ritblat Tube, would have had a smile on their faces when Pulp played Sheffield City Hall that winter, headliners in their own right so imagine the sensation of seeing Pulp top the bill at Sheffield Arena.

In the End Of Year polls, *Different Class* was voted Album Of 1995 in *Select* magazine, the *Guardian* newspaper and *Melody Maker*, the latter making it a joint favourite alongside Tricky's trip-hop masterpiece *Maxinquaye*. 'An extraordinary record,' the review opened. 'Transcending its subjects (sex and class), its times (Britpop) and its inspiration (Serge Gainsbourg, Tamla Motown, Busby Berkeley, Giorgio Moroder and The Sex Pistols) it at once summed up all that has been good this year while inadvertently revealing the inadequacies of other contenders. Pop at its best; savage and compassionate, pensive and energizing. A classic of its times and a classic for all times. Genius.'

Melody Maker also made 'Common People' Single Of The Year, calling it 'an inverse National Anthem from the moment it left Cocker's spindly fingers'.

Quite a year, then . . .

'When they write the histories of our century,' *Melody Maker* ventured, '1995 will be referred to simply as 'Pulp'. No band in living memory has dominated a calendar so completely. Jarvis Cocker has been on the front of every periodical in the world apart from the Dallas-based *Militant No-Nonsense Kick-Ass Grunge Recidivist Week*, and he has guested on every television programme bar *Blind Date*, which he will almost certainly end up hosting in his dotage.'

16

there is such a thing as a happy ending

'There's no use setting your sights on fast cars because if you do get famous, within the first week you can have both and you've got no driving force anymore, so you might as well set your sights stupidily high so that you've always got something to work to.' (Jarvis in 1985.)

'If you spend ten years of your life doing something that you think is good but nobody else seems to agree,' Jarvis pondered in 1995, 'on dark nights, you do have doubts about whether you've got it all wrong, and you're rubbish. I'll probably turn into a right bastard now'. (Jarvis in 1995.)

Wayne Furniss: dental technician and ongoing member of Sheffield band The Absolute. Peter Dalton: recovering member of the Nine O'Clock Church ('I'm just starting to get my own opinions and beliefs back,' he says, audibly relieved) and hoping for a new career in music business PR. Jamie Pinchbeck: disappeared without trace. Jarvis Cocker: of the original schoolboy hopefuls that found themselves stars of John Peel's legendary show, what else could the most pop-obsessed boy of them all do but do it his way?

At the end of the day, Jarvis decided, the prolonged delay in success has been a good thing because the group were forced to live in the real world. 'The fact that we know we can survive doing that even though it wasn't so great, means that, unlike people who've got famous when they're eighteen or something, we can fall back on real life.'

But having got used to personal space over the years, what of fame's sometime fatal pressures? The claustrophobic intrusion of privacy? Being mobbed by fans, having to negotiate the use of a bodyguard – how strange must this all feel? As Jarvis told the *NME*: 'I hate it when you have to be protected from anyone who hasn't been vetted by the management. Most of the best things that have happened in my life have come from meeting new people by surprise. I love going out and talking to people, because it makes me forget myself. To tell you the truth, I honestly don't like myself much. I bore the crap out of myself, I really do. I'd much rather be around other people. I had enough time for self-contemplation when I was on the dole, and I can't be doing with it now. So not being able to go out really scares me. I think that's when things start going wrong for famous people. You tend to turn your thoughts inward.'

Old enough to be some of his fans' father, experienced enough to know the pitfalls of celebrity, sharp enough to know that selling out in any shape or form would spoil his spotless record, believing that he has come too far now to lose sight of where he is going . . . Pulp has been the vehicle by which Jarvis Cocker has altered his life but has success changed Jarvis Cocker?

According to Russell, who should know: 'There's been no discernible change. Although, to be honest, I don't have that much to do with Jarvis these days other than working. But if you're asking if he's got all big-headed or arrogant, I think the answer is, he always was. I don't regard that as a massive fault, as he's entitled to have an ego, and he certainly has got one. Obviously he spends a lot of time on his appearance, but he always has done, in a fastidious way. He has kind of changed in a way in that it becomes inevitable that you start to feel more distant from what's going on. When you're in a small band together, in a garage, it seems more important, more crucial, whereas now you can take it or leave it to a certain extent.'

Not that Jarvis has changed in the slightest. 'His stage persona, that's him, 'cos he's never offstage,' Russell maintains. 'I've never seen him not be Jarvis. I lived with him for some period of time, and I kind of expected him to have an offstage persona, but he's just more himself onstage than off. He vibes himself up and gets cocky – you can see him backstage, shouting . . .'

Has success changed any of Pulp? Nick reckons it hasn't. 'Jarvis acts the same as he always does, he doesn't switch off, and always arses around all the time, and none of us have our own individual limousines yet. We've all got our feet on the ground-*ish*. We also argue less now than we used to.'

In Candida's eyes, Jarvis hasn't changed, he has simply got to where he has always wanted to be. 'Although he might regret it a bit now 'cos a lot is being asked of him,' she thinks.

What about herself? 'I don't want to start behaving like a pop star. I like to keep hold of reality. If it all ended I could be left there thinking, "Who am I?"' With a house bought in London and more money than she'd ever had before, success had yet to show a downside. 'The better you do, the more confident you get, so you play better, or act more like you should be there. But it's funny. "Common People" got to number two, and it's easy to get used to it, and take it for granted. We should be celebrating every day 'cos of all those years of lugging your equipment, and getting home at four in the morning, and carrying it all up those flights of stairs. Now we do *Top Of The Pops* regularly, and you get blasé. I think it's because it happens so quickly so we've not had the chance to stand back and take it all in, and think, "God, it's brilliant". It's become the norm.'

Which leads us on to the most ironic fact of all – that Pulp, those perennial misfits, have also become the norm. And ironically enough, Jarvis admits it's what he wanted all along. 'Because I felt quite an outsider when I was younger. Starting from when I first went to school in lederhosen, which set me aside in the playground, I've always wanted to be become part of the mainstream, and be accepted. But without changing.'

About the only visible change in Jarvis' behaviour has been eschewing beer for whisky or brandy – not a sign of class-upgrading but simply to save getting fat (as if). His clothes sensibility has been slightly tweaked, but even here, despite designer Katherine Hamnett putting in a special request to Jarvis to see her new collection (so that he would be, in effect, promoting anything he was keen on wearing) or Jarvis adoring the red Gucci shoes he donned for a fashion shoot and the ones with the silver buckle and fastener he didn't get the chance to model, he still favours the tweed jacket and corduroys.

No, it's unlikely that Jarvis will exchange Oxfam for *La Dolce Vita*, any more than he will turn his back on Sheffield or exploit his TV fame by advertising cars or floor cleaner or National Health specs. But as he admits, he was hardly in Sheffield this year, and a normal life seems very far away. Jarvis told *Melody Maker* that he dreamt of fixing his car – changing the old filter and replacing the brake lights, basically. After all this time, admirably so, Jarvis still has his Hillman Imp.

So is the only danger the future? If *His 'N' Hers* commemorated the 70s and *Different Class* the 80s, what about the next album?

Will Pulp, no spring chickens in pop's scheme of things, tire of touring and the consistent pressures of a top-of-the-pops life, or is there a risk of Jarvis simply going through the motions as far as his stage antics are concerned because everyone expects him to perform that way? Now that Spitting Image have given Jarvis the ultimate accolade by making a Jarvis puppet, will he look at it and think, 'is that what I'm like?'?

Now that Billy Liar has got off the train in London, but gone against the grain by making it in the big wide world – what's next, big man?

Certainly not what he was expecting At 1995's Brit Awards, the annual British music industry shindig, Jarvis admitted he got royally hammered: 'There's about three hours missing from when I was there,' he told *Vox*. At 1996's annual gathering, held

The ultimate accolade: Spitting Image celebrates the new King of Pop
(*Channel 4*)

at Earl's Court arena on 19 February, he went just that little bit further. Having performed 'Sorted For E's And Wizz' on the night, Pulp had shifted backstage during Michael Jackson's much-heralded appearance, miming to 'Earth Song' and acting like a stricken Messiah among a gaggle of children disguised as 'deprived' Third Worlders and a few adults in similar ragamuffin garb. Jarvis, Candida and Peter Mansell were standing to the side of the stage, and, egged on by Mansell, Jarvis decided to launch himself on to the stage, flicking V-signs and waggling his arse at the dinner-suited crowd and generally running amok.

In a moment of pure, hysterical farce, a man dressed as a monk revealed himself to be a bouncer and attempted to get Jarvis off the stage but Jarvis was able to evade him and returned to the wings, and then to his table. It could have been all over but, to his obvious surprise, Jarvis was subsequently arrested (as he was trying to leave) for apparent assault on sundry children and was only released on bail from Kensington Police Station at 3 a.m. the next morning without charge (though they reportedly felt it necessary to conduct a strip search; Jarvis claimed afterwards that the cell was quite comfortable, with a flushing toilet). Extraordinary – one minute he is wearing second hand threads in Sheffield, the next he's a prospective media star criminal, meeting bail conditions and back on the front of the dailies for the second time in five months.

Ironically, *Melody Maker*'s cover that week trailed an interview with Jarvis with the headline 'The Tabloids Are Out To Get Me', even before the Jarvis vs. Jacko debacle had occurred (Jarvis' comment was in reference to the attempted drug planting), but he was hardly falling short of giving them reason to explode in mock outrage. 'JACKO PULPS LOUT COCKER' blasted the *Daily Mirror*. 'BRIT STAR'S JACKO STUNT' was the *Sun*'s milder reaction. In tabloid terms, Jarvis had already turned into a right bastard, or even the devil incarnate against the Godstar Jackson, and both dailies took much pleasure in confirming Pulp won no awards that night (the group had been nominated for best album, best single and best video).

In his defence, Jarvis released a statement the next day. 'My actions were a form of protest at the way Michael Jackson sees himself as some Christ-like figure with the power of healing. The music allows him to indulge his fantasies because of his wealth and power. People go along with it even though they know it's a bit sick. I just couldn't go along with it. It was a spur of the moment decision brought on by boredom and frustration. I just ran on the stage and showed off . . . all I was doing was trying to make a point and do something lots of other people would have loved to have done if only they'd dared.'

In other words, he was acting on behalf of 'us' again. Hurrah! Pop music is a serious venture and Michael Jackson shouldn't be allowed to turn into a shallow Hollywood spectacle. All right!

It was hard to decide which was funnier – Michael Jackson

playing Jesus Christ Superstar for real, Jarvis drunkenly baiting the crowd, tabloid reports of tiny children claiming he stamped on their feet and parents insisting their child's night/life/future was ruined, or best of all, twelve-year old Ashley Moore's claim in the *Mirror* that she was picked up and nearly hurled off the stage. Jarvis can barely hold his microphone!

Jackson, meanwhile, had said (through a PR mouthpiece) that he was 'sickened, saddened, shocked, upset, cheated and angry,' as any forgiving Messiah would be. But his claim that Jarvis had 'attacked' children riled our man, and Jarvis' press statement the following day demanded an apology, claiming in turn that video evidence of the incident refuted Jackson's comments.

To show the huge impact that the pop industry – and Britpop in particular – has had in the UK, the media reaction was huge. The tabloids were joined by weekly broadsheets, mostly filled with supportive comments from different quarters – the public, the music industry and artists too, like Eno, who won the Brits producers award. *Melody Maker* and *NME* put Jarvis on the cover – the latter for the second week, having allowed Jarvis to 'edit' the previous week's issue. The *NME* printed up 'Jarvis is innocent' T-shirts, which members of the band posed in.

The irony of the spectacle was extraordinary. Jackson, who once faced charges of child abuse, serious ones that ended with a $21 million out-of-court settlement, was conspiring to see that justice be done when a cultural assailant like Jarvis might have accidentally stumbled over a tot's toe in the melée. But, as anyone sane enough could see, Jackson's Messiah-like behaviour was little less than a conspiracy to make-over his tarnished image with all the dollar-fired, self-aggrandising ballyhoo that he could muster, 'healing' children and thus the world as they hugged his glowing-white figure. 'I saw the run-through and couldn't quite believe what I was seeing then,' Jarvis told the *NME*. 'So yes, I knew what to expect. But it seemed to me that quite a lot of people there were not quite into what was going on . . . it was all being allowed to

happen because of who he was. And it was getting on my nerves
. . . sometimes you make a snap decision and you go and do something and afterwards you think that wasn't the greatest idea, but it
happened.'

It also happened right before Pulp began their arena tour.
Cynics claimed that the debacle was, in fact, a publicity stunt –
'I'm not that desperate,' Jarvis retorted. On stage at Brighton
Pavilion, where Pulp kicked off their tour, and the following night
in Cardiff, Jarvis took time to comment on the incident. 'The
thing that was bad about it,' he maintained, 'was that they said
I got in front of some children and threw them around by the
neck. I ask you, is that the sort of thing I would do?'

No, but arse-waggling is. An interview in *Q* magazine
appeared just over a week before the Brits incident, obviously
given weeks before the Brits, in which Jarvis claimed that 'the
more you show your arse at public functions, the more people
like it. The only way to disgrace yourself is by being dead boring.
It's hard not to bland out, tolerate people you shouldn't tolerate.'

Jarvis has yet to bland out. Or to let success change him. If
anything, it has energized him, kept him aware of his ideals. As he
notes, 'You have to remember that the impetus for you existing
isn't to be a celebrity and play golf with famous people.'

Not that Jarvis would have time for eighteen holes anyway.
With the arena tour a total sell-out, there was another single
to promote – 'Something's Changed', Pulp's first ballad-style
single in ten years. The latter just won out over 'F.E.E.L.I.N.G.
C.A.L.L.E.D. L.O.V.E.', and became the B-side instead, both in
remixed form and a version live from Brixton Academy, with
'Mile End' making four tracks in all.

'Mile End' was written during the *Different Class* sessions but
never used, until Pulp were asked to contribute to the soundtrack of the now hugely acclaimed *Trainspotting*. A sparse, jittery
number, its tale of Jarvis' nightmare year spent living on the
fifteenth floor of a Mile End council block, a time and place of

poverty, piss-stained lifts and desperation (*'nobody wants to be your friend 'cos "you're not from round here", as if that was something to be proud about'*) was perfect for the film's gleeful depiction of dead-end squalor.

Since *Different Class* was released, Jarvis has made the most of his star-about-town role. He was asked to duet on 'Ciao', a track on Lush's new album *Lovelife*, and on soundtrack specialist Barry Adamson's forthcoming album, while he wrote the music for *Hanging Around*, the forthcoming debut film by the art world's *enfant terrible*, sheep-pickling Damien Hirst, that Jarvis reckons doesn't sound anything like Pulp at all.

Opening the new Diesel clothes shop in London and appearing in a new Reebok TV ad doesn't sound like Jarvis either but he did, in fact, do both in March. He has yet to take up pro-celebrity golf with Tarby but Jarvis *has* become the kind of celebrity he might once have been sceptical of. That said, he is unlikely to sit on his laurels. Once the Brits furore dies down and the tour is completed, Pulp will most likely retire for a few days' holiday, but a new bout of songwriting can't be far away. From one or two comments from Jarvis, Pulp look likely to expand on the style of the last two albums. So will they become more adventurous again, acknowledging some of their earlier, darker roots? Roots that might find a whole new host of fans when, in March, surely to Pulp's chagrin and horror, Dino Records release a cut-price TV-advertised compilation of early Pulp, by the title of *Pulp Countdown 1992–1983*?

And what will be Jarvis' lyrical direction? He acknowledges that his current life consists mostly of things he wouldn't want to write songs about – money, hotels, tour fatigue, mass popularity, creature comforts in Ladbroke Grove – but, as he deadpans, 'I think I could write some quite good songs about the high life.' Or time in jail, even.

Not that Jarvis was ever really going back to jail, not after the video evidence from the Brits was investigated. 'POLICE

DECLARE JACKSON ASSAULT A PULP FICTION' was the *Guardian* lower-page front headline, reporting that Jarvis wore a pink and purple tie, a Michael Jackson fan was arrested during scuffles as Jarvis arrived at Kensington police station, and that the decision to clear him of allegations of child assault, 'was a victory for common sense'. Even the *Daily Mirror*, in classic tabloid-hypocrite mode, reversed their assault on Jarvis: '90% OF YOU BACK US IN FIGHT FOR JARVIS', it hollered, next to a picture of Simon and Yasmin Le Bon (of all old-fart rock royals!) wearing *Daily Mirror* 'Justice For Jarvis' T-shirts, as if the *Mirror* was personally fighting his case. More anti-establishment triumphs like this and Jarvis could be president in a republican 'coup' that is gathering pace as we type . . .

If everything did go wrong, then the group could always take the advice of a friend who told Jarvis, when Pulp were suffering in Sheffield, that they should learn a few covers, play the Top Rank clubs, and make some money that way. 'At the time it sounded horrible, but nowadays I think it would be quite an experience. I've always liked that sort of English cabaret thing. There's something very poignant about a big show where you can see the joins.'

Despite the polish of *Different Class*, you can still see the joins to Pulp. The niggling frustrations, the faded glamour, the small victories, the striving for brilliance but being too human to pull it off without people seeing the strain. Like pulp fiction, Pulp were once deemed cheap, trashy, gaudily coloured and ephemeral, but became something classic and collectable, something deep, something that encapsulated peoples' lives. As his Royal Jarveness reflects today, 'Things that are meaningless and throwaway often survive to define a period.' But try as he might, for all Pulp's pop antics, they are anything but meaningless and throwaway. If they were, they'd only be kitsch. And Pulp are much more than that, if only for showing that the reality of their lives, reflected in their long-overdue success, is more fantastical than any fantasy could have been.

When, in years to come, *The Jarvis Cocker Show* makes its debut, when tabloid articles are about something other than 'Revenge Of Supernerd', when Jarvis Cocker, and not Michael Jackson, is referred to as 'King of Pop', then Pulp will be seen to have been the group that defined an era. Like Blur and Oasis, the group have it in their grasp to keep progressing and fronting magazine covers when the genre has long been superseded. If pop has to be a competition, a playground scrap, the underdogs might well be the outright winners; the marginalized and disenfranchised shall inherit the earth. But, ultimately, who cares? Pop isn't a competition, or a matter of trends, as Pulp have found out. You make your own fashion. But one thing is for certain – Pulp fiction *can* have a happy ending. Russell was right – your only options *are* pop star or scrubbing crabs. Anywhere in between just wouldn't be Pulp.

discography

What Do You Say – on *Your Secret's Safe With Us* double compilation LP,
Statik STAT LP7

What Do You Say – on *The Best Of Your Secret's Safe With Us* compilation LP,
Statik STAT LP14

My Lighthouse (remix) / Looking For Life – 7" single, Red Rhino RED32

IT – mini LP, Red Rhino RED LP29 (CD reissue – Fire REFIRECD15)
My Lighthouse / Wishful Thinking / Joking Aside / Boats And Trains /
Blue Girls / Love Love / In Many Ways
* Fire CD has extra track: 'Looking For Life'

Everybody's Problem / There Was – 7" single, Red Rhino RED37

Little Girl (With Blue Eyes) – 12" EP, Fire FIRE5
Little Girl (With Blue Eyes) / Simultaneous / Blue Glow / The Will To
Power

Dogs Are Everywhere – 12" EP, Fire BLAZE10
Dogs Are Everywhere / Mark Of The Devil / 97 Lovers / Aborigine /
Goodnight

Manon (original version) – on *Imminent 4* compilation LP, Food BITE4

Don't You Know (LP version) – on *Fruitcakes And Furry Collars* compilation LP
(mail order only), *Record Mirror* RM5

They Suffocate At Night (LP version) / Tunnel – 12" single, Fire BLAZE17T

They Suffocate At Night (edit) / Tunnel (Cut Up) – 7" single, Fire BLAZE17

FREAKS – LP and CD, Fire FIRE LP5 / FIRE CD5
Fairground / I Want You / Being Followed Home / Master Of The Universe /
Life Must Be So Wonderful / There's No Emotion / Anorexic Beauty /
The Never-Ending Story / Don't You Know / They Suffocate At Night

Little Girl (With Blue Eyes) – on *The Great Fire of London* sampler LP,
Fire FIRELP8 (also on CD in Canada – RESTLESS 7-72265)

Master Of The Universe (sanitized version) / Manon (new version) / Silence – 12"
single, Fire BLAZE21T

My Legendary Girlfriend (LP version) / Is This House? / This House Is
Condemned (remixes) – 12" single, Fire BLAZE41T

Countdown (radio edit) / Death Goes To The Disco / Countdown – CD single, Fire
BLAZE51CD

Countdown / Death Goes To The Disco / Countdown (radio edit) – 12" single, Fire
  BLAZE51T

She's Dead (LP version) – on *Volume 2* compilation CD, Volume V2CD

SEPARATIONS – LP and CD, Fire 11026 (LP), Fire 33026 (CD)
  Love Is Blind / Don't You Want Me Anymore? / She's Dead / Separations /
  Down By The River / Countdown (LP version) / My Legendary Girlfriend /
  Death II / This House is Condemned

O.U. (Gone, Gone) (radio edit) / Space / O.U. (Gone, Gone) – CD single,
  Gift GIF1CD

O.U. (Gone, Gone) / Space / O.U. (Gone, Gone) (radio edit) – 12" single, Gift GIF1

My Legendary Girlfriend / Sickly Grin / Back In LA – 7" single, limited edition
  (mail order only), Caff CAFF17

Babies / Styloroc (Nites Of Suburbia) / Sheffield Sex City / Sheffield Sex City
  (instrumental) – CD single, Gift GIF3CD

Babies / Styloroc (Nites Of Suburbia) / Sheffield Sex City – 12" single, Gift GIF3

Babies (single version) – on *Indie Top 20 Volume 16* compilation LP, CD and Cassette,
  Beechwood TT016LP/CD/MC

Razzmatazz / Stacks / Inside Susan / 59 Lyndhurst Grove – CD and 12" single,
  Gift GIF6CD/GIF6

Razzmatazz / Stacks / 59 Lyndhurst Grove – 7" single, Gift 7GIF6

Razzmatazz (single version) – on *Indie Top 20 Volume 17* compilation LP, CD and
  Cassette, Beechwood TT017LP/CD/MC

PULPINTRO – THE GIFT RECORDINGS – LP, CD and Cassette, Island
  ILPM2076/IMCD159/ICM2076
  Space / O.U. (Gone, Gone) / Babies / Styloroc (Nites Of Suburbia) /
  Razzmatazz / Sheffield Sex City / Inside Susan: A Story In 3 Songs (Stacks;
  Inside Susan; 59 Lyndhurst Grove)
  * Compilation album bringing together all the Gift single tracks

Little Girl (With Blue Eyes) (single version) – on *The Indie Scene 1986* compilation
  CD, Connoisseur IBMCD86

Lipgloss (LP version) – on *You Can All Join In '94* sampler CD given free with *Vox*
  magazine, Vox CDFREE3

Lipgloss (LP version) / Deep Fried in Kelvin / You're A Nightmare – CD and
  12" single, Island CID567/12IS567

Lipgloss (LP version) / You're A Nightmare – 7" and cassette single, Island
  IS574/CIS574

Do You Remember The First Time? / Street Lites / The Babysitter – CD and 12"
  single, Island CID574/12IS574

Do You Remember The First Time? / Street Lites – 7" and Cassette single, Island
  IS574/CIS574

HIS 'N' HERS (LP, CD and Cassette) Island ILPS8026/CID8026/ICT8026
  Joyriders / Lipgloss / Acrylic Afternoons / Have You Seen Her Lately? / She's
  A Lady / Happy Endings / Do You Remember the First Time? / Pink Glove /
  Someone Like The Moon / David's Last Summer

*CD and Cassette include 'Babies' (remix) after 'Have You Seen Her Lately?'
*US CD also includes 'Razzmatazz' as a hidden bonus track

Countdown (radio edit) – on *Fire Is Good* compilation CD (mail order only), Fire
FIRECD37

The Sisters EP – CD, 12", 7", Cassette single, Island CID595/12IS595/IS595/CIS595
Babies (original version) / Your Sister's Clothes / Seconds / His 'N' Hers

MASTERS OF THE UNIVERSE – PULP ON FIRE 1985–86 – LP and CD, Fire
FIRELP36/FIRECD36
Little Girl (With Blue Eyes) / Simultaneous / Blue Glow / The Will To Power /
Dogs Are Everywhere / Mark Of The Devil / 97 Lovers / Aborigine /
Goodnight / They Suffocate At Night / Tunnel / Master Of The Universe
(sanitized version) / Manon
* Compilation album bringing together all the Fire 12" tracks, except 'Silence'

Joyriders (acoustic version) – on *Volume 10* compilation LP and CD, Volume
10VLP10/10VCD10

Do You Remember The First Time? (live version) – on *The Radio 1FM Sessions*
Cassette given free with *Vox*, Vox GIVIT8

Do You Remember The First Time? (LP version) – on *1994 Mercury Music Prize Ten*
Album Sampler compilation CD, MMPCD3

Pink Glove (LP version) – on *Really Free* compilation CD given free with *Q*
magazine, *Q*/Our Price Q99CD

Do You Remember The First Time? – on *NME Singles Of The Week 1994* mail order
compilation CD and MC, BMG 4321187012/014

Common People / Underwear – CD, 12", 7" and Cassette single, Island CID 613

Mis-Shapes / Sorted For E's And Wizz / P.T.A. (Parent Teacher Association) /
Common People (Live At Glastonbury) – CD, 12", 7" and Cassette single, Island
CID 620

Sorted For E's And Wizz / Mis-Shapes / Common People (Motiv 8 Mix) /
Common People (Vocoda mix) – CD, 12", 7" and Cassette single, Island
CIDX 620

DIFFERENT CLASS – CD, LP and Cassette, Island CID8041
Mis-Shapes / Pencil Skirt / Common People / I Spy / Disco 2000 / Live Bed
Show / Something's Changed / Sorted For E's And Wizz / F.E.E.L.I.N.G.
C.A.L.L.E.D. L.O.V.E. / Underwear / Monday Morning / Bar Italia

Disco 2000 (7" mix) / Disco 2000 (Album Mix) / Ansaphone / Live Bed Show
(Extended) – CD, 12", 7" and Cassette single, Island CID623

Disco 2000 (Album Mix) / Disco 2000 (7" mix) / Disco 2000 (Motiv8 Discoid
Mix) / Disco 2000 (Motiv8 Gimp Dub) – CD, 12", 7" and Cassette single, Island
CID623X

Something's Changed / Mile End/ F.E.E.L.I.N.G. C.A.L.L.E.D. L.O.V.E. (Moloko
Mix) / F.E.E.L.I.N.G. C.A.L.L.E.D. L.O.V.E. (Live) – CD, 12', 7' and Cassette
single, Island CID632 (Girl Sleeve), CID632X (Boy Sleeve)

fab 208